SLAVERY
SEGREGATION
AND
SCRIPTURE

"Racism is based on a profound misunderstanding of culture, of learning, and of the biology of the human species."

—SHERWOOD L. WASHBURN
in "The Study of Race,"
American Anthropologist,
LXV, 3 (1963), 528

SLAVERY SEGREGATION AND SCRIPTURE

by

JAMES O. BUSWELL, III

William B. Eerdmans Publishing Company
Grand Rapids, Michigan

To Kathleen

PREFACE

During these years of the one-hundredth anniversary of various phases of the Civil War certain outstanding parallels between slavery and racial segregation come to mind.

For example, the Negro's slave status of yesterday find its parallels in modern "caste" and color lines of today, and the social revolution that culminated in the Civil War has its counterparts in the social revolution of our day that culminated in the Supreme Court ruling against racial segregation in the public schools.

The parallels focused upon in the present study arise from the underlying racist position that has been used to support slavery and racial segregation alike. More particularly, the arguments from Scripture and from science will here be discussed.

A course on "The Negro in the New World" offered in the Graduate School at Columbia University helped to provide background material for this book. It was the teacher of this course, Dr. Charles Wagley, Professor of Anthropology, whose remarks concerning the "slaveholders' dilemma" (see pp. 26-36), stimulated the train of thought from which this study resulted. To him I am indebted for a valuable overview of the history of the Negro in the Americas.

Appreciation is also due William B. Eerdmans, Jr. for valuable suggestions for revision; Calvin Bulthuis for detailed editorial preparation and advice; Kenneth A. Lohf, Assistant Librarian of Special Collections, Columbia University, for bibliographical information; and Sheryl Weeks, Mary Spradley, and Evelyn Roberts for secretarial assistance. My wife, Kathleen Witmer Buswell, gave valuable assistance throughout, typing the first draft as well as revised portions, and smoothing out rough spots in the text.

—JAMES O. BUSWELL, III

Wheaton, Illinois

CONTENTS

7

ACKNOWLEDGMENTS

The following publishers kindly granted permission to quote from their copyrighted works indicated in the bibliography, to the extent shown in the body of this book: *Atlantic Monthly;* Ballantine Books; *The Baptist Bulletin; Defender;* Harper & Row; Macmillian Company; *Montgomery Advertiser; The New York Times; Newsweek;* Putnam's & Coward-McCann; Sheed & Ward; *U.S. News & World Report;* University of North Carolina Press; The Viking Press.

Part I

SLAVERY

INTRODUCTION

In 1847 Cyrus Pitt Grosvenor wrote that

> a Baptist minister of the South has denounced the speaking against slavery as a "sin against the Holy Ghost." On the other hand, the imputation of slavery to God, as its author, or institutor, or approver, has been declared to be "blasphemy" by too many to be enumerated.[1]

In our own day that issue is settled, only to have its place taken by another. Thus we find many who would agree with T. B. Maston, insisting that "there is no valid biblical or theological defense for the [racial] segregation pattern."[2] But we also find a great number agreeing with another "minister of the South" who insists just as strenuously that to use the Scripture to justify desegregation "is just plain blasphemy of the Bible."[3] Each group thinks its own position is certainly the right one, and the opposite view the wrong one, with varying degrees of sincerity, intelligence

[1] Cyrus Pitt Grosvenor, *A Review of the "Correspondence" of Messrs. Fuller and Wayland on the Subject of American Slavery*, 1847, p. 21.
[2] T. B. Maston, *Segregation and Desegregation: A Christian Approach*, 1959, p. 100.
[3] E. Q. Campbell and T. R. Pettigrew, *Christians in Racial Crisis: A Study of Little Rock's Ministry*, 1959, p. 45.

9

and ignorance exhibited by both. Few are willing to admit, as one defender of slavery did, the importance of

> our education, or the preconceived opinions we bring with us to the Bible, if we examine it at all; by which its teachings are prejudged and made to speak a language in unison with such education or opinion, either for or against, as the case may be. . . .[4]

So dependent was slavery upon its biblical justification in the 1850s that John Bachman, a Lutheran minister from Charleston, viewed the current "denial of the veracity of the historical Scriptures" by even pro-slavery scientists as "more dangerous to our institutions than all the ravings of the abolitionists."[5] Indeed, one anti-slavery observer admitted that his case had to appeal "solely to the Bible, because it is by such an appeal that the advocates of slavery endeavour to defend the system."[6] The extent to which this was true can be gained from his enumeration of it:

> In popular speeches; in sermons; in the solemn acts of Presbyteries, synods, conventions, conferences, and assemblies; in formal treatises . . . in pamphlets and reviews, . . . in popular illustrations . . . in newspaper articles, in learned commentaries, and in the formal opinions of erudite professors at the North and the South, . . . appeal is constantly made to the Sacred Scriptures.[7]

Segregationists today are not quite as preoccupied with the Scriptures. Nevertheless, in the habitual pattern of arguments advanced in defence of segregation, there are a significant number of striking parallels, as we shall presently discover.

---

[4] Thomas J. Taylor, "Essay on Slavery; As Connected with the Moral and Providential Government of God; and as an Element of Church Organization," 1851, p. 45.

[5] W. S. Jenkins, *Pro-Slavery Thought in the Old South*, 1935, p. 273.

[6] Albert Barnes, *In Inquiry into the Scriptural Views of Slavery*, 1846, p. 28.

[7] *Ibid.*

One of the reasons for the similarities is the high degree
to which Southern culture has had integrated within it,
first the institution of slavery, and then the special patterns
of racial segregation which have developed from that institution. W. S. Jenkins found as "the primary conclusion
resulting from the study" of *Pro-Slavery Thought in the
Old South,* "that the Southern mind was absorbed in making a defense of slavery." He goes on to point out that
although the Southern way of life was a complex and rich
civilization, it was "so completely identified with slavery
as to make its very existence seem to depend upon the
defense of that institution."[8] If we substitute "segregation"
for "slavery" and put it in the present tense, the same
observation can be made today from the literature of the
white Citizens' Councils in any city one might choose. In
fact, this has been noticeably the case, off and on, for the
better part of the past eighty years. In 1909, for example,
one writer made almost the same comparison as he noted
the marked preoccupation with a defensive system:

> Every system of oppression seeks to justify itself. The
> institutions of slavery ransacked science, history, literature,
> and religion in quest of fact and argument to uphold the
> iniquitous system. There is almost an exact parallel between
> the methods employed in support of human slavery and
> those that are now being resorted to in justification of the
> decrees of "social equality."
>
> We are told that the separation of the races is ordained
> of God, just as slavery used to be called a "divine institu-
> tion."[9]

[8] Jenkins, *op. cit.,* p. vii.
[9] Kelly Miller, *Race Adjustment: Essays on the Negro in America,*
1909, p. 115.

1

SCRIPTURAL JUSTIFICATION FOR SLAVERY

The scriptural justification for slavery took several forms, clearly defined and usually in the same patterns or combinations of arguments. These arguments can be divided into four groups: (a) general assertions that the institution was natural, "ordained of God," and of benefit to the enslaved; (b) examples of slavery described or alluded to in the Bible, chiefly in the Old Testament; (c) instructions regarding behavior of slaves and masters, chiefly in the New Testament; and (d) underlying the whole structure of the defense system (and constituting the major basis for the scriptural defense of racial segregation since post-emancipation times), the supposed teachings regarding the Negro race, chiefly based upon elaborations on the story of Ham and the curse of Noah. From the document which is "probably the first written defense of slavery in American history"[1] by one John Saffin in the year 1701, to the end of the 19th century, the same four groups of arguments are offered in one combination or another. The Church in many quarters viewed slavery as an institution, "with which ecclesiastical judicatories have not the smallest right to interfere; and in relation to which any such inter-

[1] Jenkins, *op. cit.*, p. 4.

ference . . . would be morally wrong."[2] Thus the American Anti-Slavery Society observed in their "Resolutions" of May 7, 1844, that "no institution is more hostile to the Anti-Slavery movement, than the professedly Christian Church in this country."[3]

(a) *Slavery of divine origin; of benefit to the enslaved; the natural order*

Slavery was considered to be "by Divine Appointment,"[4] "a Divine institution,"[5] "a moral relation,"[6] "God's institution,"[7] and "not immoral" but "founded in right."[8] Trevor Bowen writes that in South Carolina the Society for the Advancement of Christianity published a tract which read, "No man or set of men in our day, unless they can produce a new revelation from Heaven, are entitled to pronounce slavery as wrong. Slavery as it exists at the present day is agreeable to the order of Divine providence."[9]

Not only was the institution of slavery given Divine sanction, but the slave trade itself and the entire destiny of heathen Africans being brought to America was considered "legal,"[10] "licit,"[11] "in accordance with humane principles and

---

2 "The Charleston Union Presbytery," quoted by Barnes, *op. cit.*, p. 31.

3 Walter Clarke, "The Anti-Slavery Society at War with the Church," 1844.

4 J. C. Postell (1836), quoted by Barnes, *op. cit.*, p. 107.

5 David Ewart, *A Scriptural View of the Moral Relations of African Slavery*, 1859, p. 12.

6 *Ibid.*

7 Virginia spokesman in the House of Representatives, quoted in Trevor Bowen, *Divine White Right. A Study of Race Segregation and Interracial Cooperation in Religious Organizations and Institutions in the United States*, 1934, p. 110.

8 E. D. Sims, quoted in Barnes, *op. cit.*, p. 29.

9 Bowen, *op. cit.*, p. 107.

10 E. D. Sims, *loc. cit.*

11 R. Harris, "Scriptural Researches on the Licitness of the Slave-Trade, Shewing its Conformity with the Principles of Natural and Revealed Religion," 1788.

the laws of revealed religion,"[12] and "a merciful visitation"[13] on the grounds that it was the means of their hearing the the Gospel. *The Southern Literary Messenger* of January, 1835, carried the statement that slavery

> has done more to elevate a degraded race in the scale of humanity, to tame the savage, to civilize the barbarous, to soften the ferocious, to enlighten the ignorant, and to spread the blessings of Christianity among the heathen than all the missionaries that philanthropy and religion have ever sent forth.[14]

Similarly Samuel A. Cartwright wrote that "to expect to civilize or Christianize the negro without the intervention of slavery is to expect an impossibility."[15]   Even the great evangelist George Whitefield, writing to none other than John Wesley, in 1751, reasons that "though liberty is a sweet thing to such as are born free, yet to those who may never know the sweets of it, slavery perhaps may not be so irksome."   He admits that "I should think myself highly favored if I could purchase a good number of them, in order to make their lives comfortable, and lay a foundation for breeding up their posterity in the nurture and admonition of the Lord."[16]

Finally, slavery was widely considered to be consistent with the laws of nature.   This sentiment was expressed and implied in much of the literature of the time.   Perhaps one of the most forthright expressions is that of Dr. Cartwright:

> The same ordinance which keeps the spheres in their orbits and holds the satellites in subordination to the planets, is

[12] Thomas Thompson, *The Trade in Negro Slaves on the African Coast in Accordance with Humane Principles and with the Laws of Revealed Religion*, 1772.

[13] J. C. Postell, *loc. cit.*

[14] C. Harper, "Slavery in the Light of Social Ethics," in Elliot, ed., *Cotton is King, and Pro-Slavery Arguments*, 1860, p. 596.

[15] S. A. Cartwright, "Slavery in the Light of Ethnology," in Elliot, *op. cit.*, 1860, p. 713.

[16] Quoted in Jenkins, *op. cit.*, 42.

the ordinance that subjects the negro race to the empire of
the white man's will. Under that ordinance, our four
millions of negroes are as unalterably bound to obey the
white man's will, as the four satellites of Jupiter the superior
magnetism of that planet.[17]

(b) *Examples of slavery found in the Bible*

These could be ennumerated at some length, from the time
of Abraham to the case of Philemon, with pro and con arguments cited for each of them. However, it is our purpose
here to examine merely those arguments from Scripture which
are likewise found to be current in support of segregation.
Therefore, attention will be centered on the arguments common to both.

(c) *Instructions for slaves and masters from the New Testa-
ment*

The support for slavery from the New Testament as it was
presented by slave-owners and clergy largely centered around
the teachings found in nine references. These taught the
obedience and subservience of the slave (Titus 2:9-10;
Ephesians 6:5-9; Colossians 3:22-25; and I Peter 2:18-25),
regard for the master (I Timothy 6:1-2; Ephesians 6:5-9),
that one should remain in the state of his calling (I Corinthians 7:20-24), that a runaway slave should be returned
(Philemon), and that God intended variety in human status
(I Corinthians 12:13-26). Finally, there was an attempt to
explain away Acts 17:24-26 which the King James version
renders "God . . . hath made of one blood all nations of
men. . . ." Again, whereas an examination of the mis-
applications and certain misinterpretations on both sides might
be enlightening and worthwhile, we will not indulge in the
undertaking in this context. The Acts 17 reference will be
considered under segregation.

---

[17] Cartwright, *op. cit.*, p. 721.

(d) *Supposed teachings regarding the Negro race*

Most of the advocates of slavery, if they considered the Negro a human being, based their entire Biblical case upon the confident assumption that the Negro race must be identified as the descendants of Noah's second son, Ham. Thus, automatically, any and every mention of peoples inhabiting Egypt, Ethiopia, and the other lands occupied in the dispersal of Ham's progeny (Genesis 11) were assumed to refer to Negroes, despite the fact that these populations in historic times were non-negroid. The lengths to which pro-slavery arguments were carried to prove the association of the characteristics of negroes with Ham in order to justify the conclusion that they are under Noah's curse, were utterly fantastic.

A further assumption was constantly made that different traits of racial character correlated with Noah's three sons; furthermore, that these could be assertained by inference through Scripture. "The character given of God to each of these three sons is the character of their descendants at the present moment."[18] Thus the "descendants of Ham, the beastly and degraded son of Noah,"[19] are the characteristics of the Negro, etc. From the fact that Noah's curse involved a future of servitude for the progeny of Ham's son, Canaan, assumption was heaped upon assumption until the "logic" was impregnable. "The fact that what was said by Noah of the descendants of Ham has actually come to pass is proof positive that he did not speak [for] himself, but by the spirit of prophecy."[20] Even prominent Negro scholars have latterly given erudite expression to the acceptance of the filial relationship to Ham on the part of "the Negro who is

[18] Thornton Stringfellow, *Slavery: Its Origin, Nature and History Considered in the Light of Bible Teachings, Moral Justice, and Political Wisdom,* 1861, p. 35.

[19] *Ibid.,* p. 12.

[20] Ewart, *op. cit.,* p. 4.

his lineal descendant."[21] They, however, do not hold, that the curse upon Canaan "not only covered the person and fortunes of Ham, but that of his whole posterity also, to the very end of time"[22] which was an important element of the system of defense. It was a fundamental postulate that "African slavery is a punishment, inflicted upon the enslaved, for their wickedness."[23]

The reasoning went something like this: Ham was a word which meant "black," not only referring to his skin color but also to "the very disposition of his mind." He was characterized as having always been wicked ("cursed Ham" not "cursed be Ham")[24] with "violence of temper, exceedingly prone to acts of ferocity and cruelty, involving murder, war, butcheries, and even cannibalism, including beastly lusts, and lasciviousness . . . dishonesty, treachery, lowmindedness, and malice."[25] Josiah Priest, in his *Bible Defense of Slavery* (1852), even went so far as to presume, from a rather strained application of Leviticus 18:8, that Ham had committed "abuse and actual violation of his own mother."[26] This "group of horrors . . . couched in the word Ham" is all seen as "agreeing, in a most surprising manner, with the color of Ham's skin, as well as with his real character as a man, during his own life, as well as with that of his race, even now."[27] The curse of servitude was thus the logical outcome of sin, and served as the "very first notice of slavery upon record." It was designed by God "to be perpetuated through all time, and was intended to cement and compact the whole

[21] A. P. B. Holly, *God and the Negro: . . . or, the Biblical Record of the Race of Ham*, 1937, p. 23.

[22] Josiah Priest, *Bible Defense of Slavery; and Origin, Fortunes and History of the Negro Race*, 1852, p. 91.

[23] Howell Cobb, *A Scriptural Examination of the Institution of Slavery in the United States*, 1856, p. 3.

[24] Priest, *op. cit.*, p. 93.

[25] *Ibid.*, p. 40.

[26] *Ibid.*, p. 182.

[27] *Ibid.*, p. 40.

human family, to establish the system of mutual relation and dependency, and to sustain the great chain of subordination, so essential to the Divine, as well as all human governments."[28] Thus the curse, and thus the continuity. As a system of defense it was, and always has been, revealing of the most naive form of ethnocentrism. One writer of the period, for example, concluded:

> We see, in these people, not only mental but physical pecularities which distinguish them from all other peoples, *which pecularities suffice to show* both the extent of their wickedness and the extent of the curse of Noah's prophecy.[29]

[28] Alexander McCaine, "Slavery Defended From Scripture, Against the Attacks of the Abolitionists," 1842, p. 5.

[29] Cobb, *op. cit.*, pp. 74-75. (Italics are author's)

2

NEGRO ORIGINS

The origin of the Negroes has been the subject of much speculation, giving rise during slavery times in America to a great body of "Niggerology"[1] in which Biblical interpretations figured prominently. The theories as to Negro origins can be divided into five different sets of arguments. The first, that of presuming that the Negro differentiated slowly from the racial type of the family of Noah, was hard to support in view of the fact that the ancient Egyptians were proven to have known the Negro type by archeologists. This, within the framework of a very recent creation, resulted in the Negro being considered a permanent, "pure" type which had existed from the start. Therefore, within these considerations, other theories for his origin abounded.

The second system of argument was that the Negro was descended from Ham, and that Ham was born black.

> God . . . superintended the formation of two of the sons of Noah, in the womb of their mother, in an extraordinary and supernatural manner, giving to these children such forms of bodies, constitutions of natures, and complexions of skin as suited his will. . . .Japheth he caused to be born white, . . . while he caused Ham to be born black, a color still further removed from the red hue of his parents than was white.[2]

[1] J. C. Nott, letter of Feb. 14, 1849, quoted in Jenkins, *op. cit.*, p. 260.
[2] Priest, *op. cit.*, p. 33.

Thus Priest referred to Ham as "the gigantic negro" whose "form of body" included a "vastly different" skull, with bones "made far stronger, thicker, harder, and more compact in relation to the sutures." Compared to the white man's skull, the negro's "is nearly as firmly knit together as if there were no sutures at all, or as if the head was but one continued bone." The great thickness, he added, was a "singular providence" for the Negro as it provided him with "a powerful weapon, both of attack and defense."[3]

Another variety of this argument is that Cain, Adam's son and murderer of Abel, his brother, was punished with servitude, and that "Ham had married a descendant of Cain, thus placing a double curse upon Canaan, his son."[4] Cartwright thought that Cain himself had been turned black (making Ham's wife black, too) since it is recorded in Genesis 4:13-15 that the Lord, in answer to Cain's complaint, "set a mark upon Cain lest any finding him should kill him." Cartwright surmised that this was black skin from his observation that "The wild Arabs and hostile American Indians invariably catch the black wanderer and make a slave of him instead of killing him, as they do the white man."[5]

The third system of argument was that "the races had actually been transformed by God at the Tower of Babel by the same instantaneous fiat by which he had confounded the languages. . ."[6] It was thought that the races were thus preadapted to the lands of their ultimate habitation.

The fourth system of argument has as its basis that the Negro, although human, constituted another species of man, and that Adam was the father of only the white race.[7]

Samuel Cartwright in his essay, "Slavery in the Light of Ethnology" designated the "species Prognathous." How-

---

3 *Ibid.*, pp. 48-49.
4 Jenkins, *op. cit.*, p. 119.
5 Cartwright, *op. cit.*, p. 711.
6 Described by Jenkins, *op. cit.*, pp. 253-254.
7 *Ibid.*, p. 272.

ever, he made it clear that, "It is not intended by the use of the term Prognathous to call in question the black man's humanity or the unity of the human race as a *genus*. . . ."[8] Some of the characteristics of the species in question, according to this observer (who had spent a lifetime of "observation and experience . . . in an extensive practice of medicine in the midst of the race,"[9]) were that "the typical negro's nervous system is modelled a little different from the Caucasian and somewhat like the orangutan."[10]   Regarding skull position and posture:

> The occipital foramen, giving exit to the spinal cord . . . is so oblique as to form an angle of 30 degrees with the horizon . . . so to throw the head somewhat backward and the face upward . . . Hence, from the obliquity of the head and the pelvis, the negro walks steadier with a weight on his head, as a pail of water, for instance, than without it; whereas the white man, with a weight on his head, has great difficulty in maintaining his center of gravity, owing to the occipital foramen forming no angle with the cranium, the pelvis, the spine, or the thighs — all forming a straight line from the crown of the head to the sole of the foot. . . .[11]

Others named the Negro as the lowest order of mankind, a separate species in some cases,[12] the species difference not specified in many others.   Josiah Priest simply considered the Negro to be "a race totally different from whites, in every respect that can be thought of, except that they are human, but of the lowest order. . . ."[13] Jenkins refers to others who thought so[14] and there are still more.   Of particular note for

---

[8] Cartwright, *op. cit.*, p. 707.

[9] E. N. Elliot, *Cotton is King, and Pro-Slavery Arguments*, 1860, p. xiii.

[10] Cartwright, *op. cit.*, p. 709.

[11] *Ibid.*, pp. 709-710.

[12] J. H. Van Evrie, *White Supremacy and Negro Subordination; or, Negroes a Subordinate Race and Slavery its Normal Condition,* 1867, pp. 79-80. (Van Evrie designated six species corresponding almost to the modern major racial stocks.)

[13] Priest, *op. cit.*, p. 389.

[14] *Op. cit.*, p. 40.

his abysmal ignorance, yet typical arguments, is Van Evrie, who wrote in 1867 that "the Negro, if isolated by himself, seems utterly incapable of transmitting anything whatever to the succeeding generation."[15]   He claimed that the Negro's "capacities cannot go beyond the living or actual genera- tion. . . ."[16]   Perhaps his most amusing description takes a poke at the North as he portrays the Negro's body as absolute- ly incapable of erect posture:

> The head of the negro projecting posteriorly, places his eyes at an angle with the horizon, and thus alone enables him to approximate an erect position. . . .the slightest change of an elementary atom in the negro structure would render him an impossible monstrosity.   But with the broad forehead and cerebellum of the white man, it is perfectly obvious that the negro would no longer possess a centre of gravity, and therefore those philanthropic people who would "educate" him into intellectual equality or change the mental organism of the negro, would simply render him incapable of standing on his feet or of an upright position on any terms.[17]

Under this system of arguments are also found the answers to one of the plain commands of Scripture against slavery: Exodus 21:16, "And he that stealeth a man and selleth him, or if he be found in his hand, he shall surely be put to death."   Priest claims the passage does not refer to cap- turing Negroes, but only to Hebrews attempting to steal and sell other Hebrews.[18]   The more general response is one which similarly attempts to answer the Declaration of Independence statement that "all men are created equal." Paulding claimed that "the slaves of the United States have never been considered as included. . . .   They are neither comprehended in the phrase 'man', nor 'citizen . . . .'"[19]   The

---

15 Van Evrie, *op. cit.*, pp. 79-80.
16 *Ibid.*, p. 87.
17 *Ibid.*, pp. 93-94.
18 Priest, *op. cit.*, pp. 333-334.
19 J. K. Paulding, *Slavery in the United States*, 1835, p. 44.

reason is, as the Rev. Quincy Ewing has pointed out, that the white man is convinced that "he is 'not human' in the sense that he is human, not entitled to the exercise of human rights in the sense that he is entitled to the exercise of them."[20]

The fifth system of argument holds that the Negroes are not humans at all, but merely beasts. In at least two cases to be found in the literature, the form of the Negro was said to have been taken by Satan as the tempter in the Garden of Eden. Thus Ariel (pseudonym of Buckner H. Payne) claimed that "the tempter in the garden of Eden . . . was a beast, a talking beast . . . the negro."[21] Similarly, Cartwright, changing his mind about the species Prognathous being human, wrote in 1860 that he agreed with the Englishman Dr. Adam Clark who, fifty years before, had believed that the creature who tempted Eve was an orangutan. "If he had lived in Louisiana, instead of England," Cartwright suggested, "he would have recognized the *negro gardener*."[22]

The low point in the "Niggerology" of the day came with the writings of Ariel in 1840, (revised in 1867), and of Charles Carroll as late as 1900, both of whom claimed that the Negro was a beast.

According to Ariel the Negro was neither a descendant of Ham nor of Adam and Eve. "God's nomenclature of creation" included Birds, Fowls, Creeping things, Cattle, Beasts, and Adam and Eve. "Beasts" were not four-footed, but two-footed, including the apes. Since the Negro was quite definitely *not* of the family of Noah, but *is* present with us today, he must have been in the Ark. But since only Noah's family had descended from Adam, the conclusion was certain — the Negro "is inevitably a beast." He also believed that the Ne-

---

[20] Ewing, Quincy, "The Heart of the Race Problem," *Atlantic Monthly*, Vol. CIII (Mar. 1909), pp. 389-390, as quoted in H. Paul Douglass, *Christian Reconstruction in the South*, 1909, pp. vii-viii.

[21] Ariel, (B. H. Payne), *The Negro: What is His Ethnological Status?* 1867, pp. 45-46.

[22] Cited by Jenkins, *op. cit.*, p. 254.

gro has no soul. There were "eight souls" saved in the ark. They are all accounted for by Noah's family. The Negro was a beast in the ark, "consequently he has no soul to be saved."[23]

Astonishingly, however, Ariel's arguments against connection of the Negro with Ham, while shot through with fanciful logic, are essentially sound.

One strange theory that Ariel and Josiah Priest held in common, was that the Tower of Babel was built solely by Negroes.[24] Racial differentiations were not solely based on ideas about the Negro. Ariel, for instance, found it "indisputably plain" that Adam had "long, straight hair, high forehead, high nose, thin lips, and white skin." [25]

The views of Carroll included the belief that Cain married a "soulless" Negro, that his offspring were likewise soulless. He also considered the Biblical "beast" to be a biped of which the Negro was one variety. Carroll claimed in addition, however, that "the teachings of science prove the Negro an ape."[26]

Perhaps the most atrocious claims stemming from such views were those regarding inter-racial marriage. Carroll wrote of the Mulatto:

. . . these monstrosities have no rights social, financial, political, or religious that man need respect; . . . not even the right to live.

He presumed that the Mulatto is only

upon the earth in violation of Divine law. Hence it is not a part of God's creation. And there can never be any peace between God and man so long as this corrupted flesh is permitted to "defile" the earth with its presence.[27]

From the foregoing, perhaps a clearer picture can be gained as to the various scripturally-related attitudes regard-

[23] Ariel, *op. cit.*, p. 44.
[24] Priest, *op. cit.*, p. 386; Ariel, *op. cit.*, pp. 32-34.
[25] Ariel, *op. cit.*, p. 24.
[26] Charles Carroll, *"The Negro a Beast"* or *"In the Image of God . . .,"* 1900, p. 159.
[27] *Ibid.*, p. 161.

ing the inferiority of the Negro race, the ideology which was the foundation of slavery, and as to why any teaching of racial equality was considered "founded on a total ignorance of nature."[28] It amazes one that most of the authors of the day could firmly believe, as Stringfellow wrote in 1861, that "The picture drawn expresses sober historical truth with respect to Ham's sons."[29] Amidst the clamor of pro-slavery arguments on the one hand and the relentless din of fanatical abolitionists on the other the writings of enlightened authors were but a small voice. To cite but one, Cyrus Pitt Grosvenor wrote in 1847 with contempt of "this stereotyped proof of the Negro's inferiority, got up by slaveholders, — 'the curse or prophecy of Noah,' which it is high time that Whites should understand."[30] He further believed that

> so long as existing error in relation to the history of the African race, causing them to be regarded as intellectually inferior to other men, shall continue to brood upon the minds of the American people, it will be impossible to reach effectually the slaveholding conscience.[31]

We shall turn now to a consideration of the slow process of enlightenment which invaded the minds of slaves, and then masters, eventuatinng in a war, and a Supreme Court decision.

[28] Paulding, *op. cit.*, p. 65.
[29] Stringfellow, *op. cit.*, p. 12.
[30] Grosvenor, *op. cit.*, p. 139.
[31] *Ibid.*, p. 142.

3

EVANGELISM AND EDUCATION — THE SLAVERS' DILEMMA

As we have already noted, the slave trade and the institution of slavery were partially defended on the basis that the infidel Africans were thus brought under the influence of the Gospel in a Christian land. Church and missionary agencies were not slow to realize that the mounting number of slaves, particulary in the New World, constituted a ready and needy mission field of challenging proportions. However, a constant and demoralizing frustration was met with on every hand, namely, the widespread conviction that the message of Christianity was not intended for the inferior races. Bishop Berkley, after visiting the colony of Rhode Island, told the Society for the Propagation of the Gospel in Foreign Parts on February 18, 1731, "An ancient antipathy to the Indians . . . together with an irrational contempt of the Blacks, as creatures of another species, who had no right to be instructed or admitted to the sacraments; have proved a main obstacle to the conversion of these poor people."[1] Such opinions as reported by the Bishop were also held in certain church circles where preoccupation was with purity of doctrine rather than missionary outreach. One, Dr. Mc-

[1] Charles C. Jones, *The Religious Instruction of the Negroes in the United States*, 1842, pp. 28-29; Jenkins, *op. cit.*, p. 17.

Farlane, a "clearheaded, bold, and eccentric old Methodist," is reported by Cartwright as doubting the possibility of civilizing the Africans, and concluding "that the Written Word was not intended for those inferior races who can not read it."[2] Perhaps the best known statement of this kind is the rebuff received by the later renowned missionary, William Carey, shortly before his first voyage to India in 1792. At a ministerial meeting at Nottingham, he was invited to propose a topic for discussion. He suggested, "The duty of Christians to attempt the spread of the Gospel among heathen nations," whereupon the moderator replied, "Young man, sit down! When God pleases to convert the heathen, He will do it without your aid or mine."

Despite sentiment of this kind, activity was going on toward the evangelization of the slave populations. In 1673 Richard Baxter had laid the foundations for converting the slaves in his *Christian Directory,* which "had an extensive circulation among the plantation owners."[3] The Church of England began to take an active interest in converting the American slaves after 1679,[4] and in 1685, one of its clergymen, Morgan Godwyn, before James II, "preached a sermon deploring the condition of the slaves and pleading that His Majesty use some endeavor toward having the Gospel ideas propagated in the Colonies."[5] The King is recorded to have made a resolution the same year, "that the negroes in the Plantations should all be baptised."[6]

In 1701 under William III, the Society for the Propagation of the Gospel in Foreign Parts was incorporated, with three great objectives: "the care and instruction of our people settled in the Colonies; the conversion of the Indian Savages;

[2] Cartwright, *op. cit.,* p. 715.
[3] Jenkins, *op. cit.,* p. 13.
[4] Bowen, *op. cit.,* p. 90.
[5] Jenkins, *op. cit.,* p. 14.
[6] J. Evelyn, Diary entry for Sept. 16, 1685; quoted in Jenkins, *op. cit.,* p. 14.

and the conversion of the Negroes."[7]   A good many missionaries were thus directed to considerable activity among the American slaves.

"In 1723 a group known as 'Associates of Doctor Bray,' which included Benjamin Franklin among its members, came into being with the special aim of giving religious instruction to Negroes."[8]

The following year, the French "Code Noir" included a passage "which obliged every planter to have his Negroes baptized and properly instructed in Christianity."[9]

Opposition of various kinds was making the task of evangelizing the American slaves increasingly complex.   Nevertheless, revivals swept certain areas in the 1740s, as they did almost a hundred years later; and Negro church membership increased steadily.   Negro Methodist membership was listed at 1,890 in 1786, and rose to 11,682 in 1790.   Three years later it was 16,277.[10]   Other denominations increased accordingly. In 1773 the first Negro Baptist church was founded, and in 1794 at Savannah, Georgia, another one began after many persecutions.   It very soon had a membership of over 700.[11] An indication of Negro attendance at white churches is the fact that the first separate gallery for slaves was introduced by the Cumberland Street Methodist Church of Charleston in 1787.[12]

It is necessary to pause at this point to consider the profound influence which the evangelistic effort had upon slavery, the dilemma which persistantly faced the slave owner, and his successive attempts to resolve it.

The great dilemma, which existed from the beginning of slavery in the New World until the Civil War, was the

[7] Jones, *op. cit.*, p. 9.
[8] Bowen, *loc. cit.*
[9] *Ibid.*, p. 88.
[10] *Ibid.*, p. 93.
[11] *Ibid.*, p. 93-94.
[12] *Ibid.*, p. 96.

fundamental opposition of the principles of Christianity to the institution of slavery itself. For the slaveholder it took form initially in the stark question as to whether or not the conversion or baptism of his slave (which many had considered "soulless") necessitated any change in his status as a slave. There was ample reason for the confusion thus precipitated by such conversions in a history of legal and ideological precedent not to be overthrown lightly: "The English colonists had to overcome the difficulty found in the observance of the law that no Christian could be held a slave."[13] Even the religious slaveholders who had entered into the relationship with earnest missionary motives, had their religious zeal "tempered by the conviction that neither Christian brotherhood nor the law of England would justify the slavery of Christians."[14]

The background of the matter lay in the comparatively ancient conviction that it was permissable to enslave the heathen. This stemmed, in part, from the belief that slavery was the natural consequence of the sin of the enslaved and that it was ordained by the judgement of God. The question is discussed by Jenkins,[15] who points out various cases in which this viewpoint actually obtained legal sanction. Coke's opinion in Calvin's case in 1608 is cited: "He layed down the rule that infidels were perpetual enemies which might be killed, or, in lieu thereof, be made perpetual prisoners or slaves . . . for the law presumes not that they will be converted, that being *remota potentia* (a remote possibility)." In 1677 a court held "that *negroes* . . . being infidels, there might be a property in them sufficient to maintain trover. . . ." And in 1694 a similar case involving ". . . a negro boy, for they are heathens, and therefore a man may have property in them. . . ."

[13] C. G. Woodson, *The Education of the Negro Prior to* 1861, 1915, p. 24.
[14] Bowen, *op. cit.*, p. 8.
[15] Jenkins, *op. cit.*, pp. 18-19.

The idea that conversion to Christianity should result in actual freedom seems to have stemmed, formally, (though there is a greater emphasis upon the strength of the popular belief or custom) from the ancient common law stating that "Villains become free many ways; some by baptism, as those *Saracans* [sic] who are taken by Christians or bought, and brought to Christianity by grace."[16] Later, in the year 1677, there is a case on record in which one of the arguments involved 100 Negroes who were to "go to the administrator until they become Christians; and thereby they are enfranchised."[17]

Thus it is not hard to understand the reaction of slaveholders who, for the better part of two hundred years, were, in varying degrees, hostile to the advances of Christianity toward their slaves.

Parallel with this conviction, however, were the many insistent denials by spokesmen of high and low estate, both formally and informally, publically and privately, stating that manumission was not compulsory upon conversion or baptism.   Thus one, John Evelyn, in a diary entry for September 16th, 1685 considered it "a mistaken opinion" that baptised slaves "would be *ipso facto* free,"[18] while Bishop Berkeley, before the Society for the Propagation of the Gospel in Foreign Parts in 1731, considered it "an erroneous notion."[19] Indeed, such was the crucial nature of the question that specific legislation was forthcoming in an attempt to provide freedom of evangelism along with salve for the consciences of slave owners. As early as 1667 the colony of Virginia passed a law, referred to by Paulding in 1836 as "a curious ancient statute" stating that "the conferring of baptism doth not alter the condition of the person as to his bondage or freedom, to the end that masters, freed from this doubt, may more care-

---

[16] *Ibid.*, p. 20.
[17] *Ibid.*
[18] Quoted, *Ibid.*, p. 14.
[19] Jones, *op. cit.*, p. 28.

fully endeavour the propagation of Christianity. . . ."[20] In 1671 Maryland provided that "the conversion of the Holy Sacrament of Baptism does not alter the status of slaves or their issue."[21] Other statutes to the same effect were passed in Virginia in 1682 and 1705, Maryland in 1699, New York in 1706, 1788, and 1801.[22]

One of the most detailed attempts to further the propagation of the Gospel among the American slaves was a lengthy letter prepared by the Bishop of London, addressed "to the Masters and Mistresses of Families in the English Plantations abroad; exhorting them to encourage and promote the Instruction of their Negroes in the Christian Faith." This letter, dated in London, 1727, provided explicitly for the dilemma under consideration:

> Christianity and the embracing of the Gospel does not make the least alteration in civil property, or in any of the duties which belong to civil relations; but in all these respects, it continues persons just in the same state as it found them. The freedom which Christianity gives is a freedom from the bondage of sin and satan, and from the dominion of men's lusts and passions and inordinate desires; but as to their outward *condition,* whatever that was before, whether bond or free, their being baptized and becoming Christians, makes no manner of change in it. As St. Paul has expressly told us, I Cor. 7:20, where he is speaking directly to this point, "Let every man abide in the same calling wherein he was called:" and at the 24th verse, "Let every man wherein he is called therein abide with God.[23]

Although this and many other expressions of like content were intended to ease the tension and provide official resolution to the dilemma, the anticipated results were not forth-

---

[20] Paulding, *op. cit.,* p. 147.
[21] Jesse B. Barber, *Climbing Jacob's Ladder. The Story of the Work of the Presbyterian Church, U. S. A., Among the Negroes,* 1952, p. 12.
[22] Jenkins, *op. cit.,* p. 22.
[23] Quoted in Jones, *op. cit.,* pp. 21-22.

coming. History reveals most clearly that the dilemma was not limited merely to the question of conversion and automatic manumission. To learn its real nature we must examine the subsequent reactionary tactics and rationlizations on the part of the 18th and 19th century slaveowners.

The Reverend James Ramsay, in his *Essay on the Treatment and Conversion of African Slaves* published in 1784, relates how he was rebuffed by the slaveowners "on his first settlement as a minister in the West Indies" in 1766. After making public attempts to instruct the slaves, inviting them to his meetings and inviting their masters to send them, he reported (writing in the third person):

> But inconceivable is the listlessness with which he was heard, and bitter was the censure heaped on him in return. It was quickly suggested, and generally believed, . . . that he aimed at making of them Christians, to render them incapable of being good slaves. . . .
>
> No master would use any influence with his slaves to make them attend at the appointed hours. . . .
>
> In bidding prayer, he had inserted a petition for the conversion of slaves. It was deemed so disagreeable a memento,. that several white people, on account of it, left off attending divine service. He was obliged to omit the prayer entirely, to try and bring them back.[24]

In a similar account, Bishop Asbury, in a journal entry for February 1, 1809, wrote:

> We are defrauded of great numbers by the pains that are taken to keep the blacks from us. Their masters are afraid of the influence of our principles.[25]

It is in this statement that we find the crux of the matter. Exactly what were these "principles" and what was their "influence" of which the masters were afraid? The testimony of time has confirmed the convictions of men like Albert Barnes who saw that Bible doctrine constituted a "strike at

[24] James Ramsay, *An Essay on the Treatment and Conversion of African Slaves in the British Sugar Colonies,* 1784, pp. 178-180.
[25] Quoted in Jenkins, *op. cit.,* p. 15.

one of the fundamental conceptions on which slavery is based — the essential superiority of one class of men over another."[26] Writing in 1846, Barnes ably and dispassionately presented the argument against slavery based on the doctrine of human equality "which lies everywhere on the face of the Bible." If it were not for the belief in the inferiority of the Negro, he argued, "slavery could not long exist at all." The moment when belief in racial inferiority disappears, and racial equality takes its place in men's minds, that all are equal under God, "that moment a death-blow will be given to slavery, from which it will never recover." Human inequality "receives no countenance from the New Testament."[27]

The Bible teachings were correctly seen, not as explicitly striking at slavery as such, for it would have been inconsistent to precipitate the kind of social turmoil which would inevitably have followed. The Bible was given in a particular language and in a real culture, and its presentation, though not its content, had to be adapted, the same as it must be on any mission field today, to the receiving culture. The consequences of receiving the Gospel work revolution directly only in the individual; and, through the individual's changed values, indirectly in the society. The defenders of slavery saw only the existing culture of Bible times reflected in its pages and assumed that since slavery was included, the institution thus received divine sanction. The effect of the Gospel upon slavery, however, was correctly seen by others as a process of changing human values, and thus working a social revolution through a period of time. Barnes referred to "its mild and gentle influence" which "would ultimately abolish the system."[28]

It was the combination of many teachings which, together,

[26] Barnes, op. cit., pp. 312-313.
[27] Ibid. Barnes (pp. 272-313) gives the best presentation of the scripturally-based arguments against slavery and racial inequality.
[28] Ibid., p. 366.

resulted inevitably in a doctrine subversive to slavery. Charles
Jones reported in 1842 the masters' accusations, that

> you teach them that "God is no respector of persons:"
> that "he hath made of one blood all the nations of men;"
> "thou shalt love thy neighbor as thyself;" "all things what-
> soever ye would that men should do to you, do ye even so
> to them. . . ."[29]

It was no wonder to many that their was objection to instruction in the Scriptures. For, as Barnes reported, the slaveholders were only too well aware of its influence on their
slaves, as well as its distaste to their own consciences, in
many cases. He wrote, "I have myself repeatedly conversed
with intelligent gentlemen of the slaveholding states on the
subject, and I have never seen one who did not admit that
the gospel would ultimately remove slavery entirely." Furthermore, he felt that it was undoubtedly the "belief of the
great mass of private Christians and Christian ministers" in
the South that the application of Scriptural teachings would
be effective "first to meliorate the condition of the slave, and
ultimately to effect his entire emancipation."[30]

Thus the "principles," and thus their "influence" of which
the masters were afraid. As Jones pointed out, "The objection, it will be perceived, is levelled against the *influence of
the Gospel itself.* . . ."[31]

The dilemma which faced the slaveholders is thus seen to
have been, not simply a legal matter, nor merely a matter to
be decided by ecclesiastical authority. It was the fundamental opposition of the Bible to the very foundations of
slavery, and the pressing problem of its propagation to their
slaves. The alternatives were clear. As stated by one his-
torian, the slaveholders "had either to let the institution gradually pass away or close all avenues of information to the

---

[29] Jones, *op. cit.*, p. 197.
[30] Barnes, *loc. cit.*
[31] Jones, *op. cit.*, p. 194.

minds of their Negroes."[32]   The successive attempts, and the lengths taken to accomplish the second alternative constitute one of the more disgraceful chapters in American social history.

[32] Woodson, *op. cit.*, p. 24.

4

SUPPRESSION OF EDUCATION

In addition to the scriptural opposition to the basic inequality of man, there were other important consequences
of religious instruction which led to the attempts to "close
all avenues of information to the minds of their Negroes." At
least six arguments are listed by Bowen[1] as figuring in one
way or another in the opposition to religious instruction:
(i) Conversion would lower the economic value of the slave
and raise the cost of keeping him. (ii) The time taken to
instruct him could not be spared. (iii) Church attendance
conflicted with Sunday labor. (iv) Religious instruction developed ideas of equality which led to dissatisfaction with
slave status. (v) This increased the danger of insurrection
and revolt. (vi) Association with Negroes on terms of
equality in church and at communion table was distasteful.

Furthermore, religious instruction always involved learning
to read, and there were other things than the Bible to read.
Literature from the West Indies, from France, and from
the Northern Abolitionists inflamed the minds of the Negroes
far beyond the ethical teachings of scripture. The religious
instruction of slaves was thus seen as leading to many sources
of general enlightenment, all of which, in one way or another,
jeopardized the institution of slavery. So the intellectual,

[1] Bowen, *op. cit.*, pp. 91-92.

emotional, and legislative defenses had to be constantly adjusted to the fluctuations in the tide of mental and moral enlightenment of the slaves. The surest way to prevent any of the consequences of instruction was to prevent the slaves from learning to read.

The methods of the defense builders toward this end were heralded by their reaction to the early Quaker movements for the benefit of the Negroes. This religious group was active from the earliest colonial days, and in 1696 "while protesting against the slave trade, denounced also the policy of neglecting their moral and spiritual welfare."[2] Woodson reports that in 1713 they had "a definite scheme for freeing and returning them to Africa after having been educated and trained to serve as missionaries on that continent." But they "soon found themselves at war with the leaders of the time,"[3] and "incurred the ill will of the masters who denounced them as undesirable persons, bringing into America spurious doctrines subversive of the institutions of the aristocratic settlements."[4] In 1672 they passed a law prohibiting Quakers from taking slaves to their meetings and, six years later, passed another law which "excluded Quakers from the teaching profession by providing that no person should be allowed to keep a school in Virginia unless he had taken the oath of allegiance and supremacy. Of course, it was inconsistent with the spirit and creed of the Quakers to take this oath."[5]

The legislative curtailing of Negro education continued with the enactment of a law against instructing slaves in South Carolina as early as 1740. Georgia, in 1770, even during a time when increased value was attached to a slave who could read and write, saw sufficient threat to her interests to reenact a 1740 law "which imposed a penalty on anyone who

---

[2] Woodson, *op. cit.*, p. 44.
[3] *Ibid.*
[4] *Ibid.*, p. 45.
[5] *Ibid.*, pp. 45-46.

should teach or cause slaves to be taught or employ them 'in any manner of writing whatever.' "[6]

With the coming of the industrial revolution and the resulting increase in the size of cotton plantations in the south, the most influential land holders found themselves using ever greater numbers of slaves. Whereas the education of the Negroes in the North, in certain urban centers in the South, and even on many plantations had been continuing hand in hand with religious instruction, the increasing number of slaves in the Cotton South was beginning to present management difficulties for the owners. This resulted in the inevitable; enlightenment had to be suppressed. "Many of the planters thus enriched, believed that the slightest amount of education, merely teaching slaves to read, impaired their value because it instantly destroyed their contentedness."[7] The industrial revolution was only one of many interwoven reasons for the marked increase in active suppression of education. However, these so converged and impressed themselves upon the slaveholding states during about the first third of the 19th century that the "avenues of information to the minds of their Negroes" were almost entirely blocked. "Slaves who were, during the eighteenth century, advertised as valuable on account of having been enlightened, were in the nineteenth century considered more dangerous than useful."[8]

Woodson's resume[9] of the stringent laws passed to control the situation reads like a totalitarian or *gestapo* idealogy usually conceived of as most foreign to the American tradition. In 1817 Missouri passed an act which barred Negroes from attending schools. In 1819 the General Assembly of Virginia passed a law "providing that there should be no more assemblages of slaves, or free Negroes, or mulattoes, mixing or

[6] *Ibid.,* p. 64
[7] *Ibid.,* p. 153.
[8] *Ibid.*
[9] *Ibid.,* pp. 159-171.

associating with such slaves, for teaching them reading or writing." Mississippi followed with a similar law in 1823. 1830 saw Louisiana pass a measure providing that

> all persons who should teach, or permit or cause to be taught, any slave to read or write, should be imprisoned not less than one month nor more than twelve.

The following year Georgia passed a similar law; Virginia extended its law to include freedmen and mulattoes; and Delaware declared that "no free Negro should attempt to call a meeting for religious worship, to exhort or preach, unless he was authorized to do so by a judge or justice of the peace, upon the recommendation of five respectable and judicious citizens."

A year later, in 1832, Alabama enacted a law "imposing a fine of from $250 to $500 on persons who should attempt to educate any Negro whatsoever"; Florida passed a law similar to that of Delaware's; and Virginia, in reaction to Nat Turner's rebellion of the previous year, proclaimed that "No Negro ordained, licensed, or otherwise, could hold religious or other assemblies at any time — day or night."[10] Also on its books was a law "that if any white person, for pay or compensation, shall assemble with any slaves for the purpose of teaching, and shall teach any slave to read or write, such person, or any white person contracting with such teacher so to act, shall be liable to a fine."[11]

Making instruction of slaves illegal was not sufficient. It was discovered that some were learning to read informally in connection with their employment. Thus Georgia set a penalty upon anyone employing any Negro "in setting up type or other labor about a printing office requiring a knowledge of reading and writing."[12] Similarly, South Carolina in 1834 "provided that persons of African blood should not be

---

[10] Bowen, *op. cit.*, p. 112.
[11] Paulding, *op. cit.*, pp. 146-178.
[12] Woodson, *loc. cit.*

employed as clerks or salesmen." The following year, North Carolina prohibited the public instruction of Negroes.

What was the reaction of the church to all of this? Charles Jones, attempting to meet the problem of converting the slaves, wrote in 1842, "Shall we speak of *access to the Scriptures?* The *statutes* of our respective slave States forbid all knowledge of letters to the Negroes; and where the statutes do not, *custom* does."[13] Thus it became a widespread custom for the white preachers, who in many cases were still permitted to address slaves on the plantations, to carry on their work with a well-planned, but strictly oral method of instruction. The institution of slavery thus made its impact upon missionary method in a manner not duplicated anywhere else on earth. It is reported that

> the Episcopal Church, for example, felt that it was no longer necessary to cultivate Negro intellects. The richest slaveholders were Episcopalians. Could the church act in a manner prejudicial to the interests of its parishoners? The Episcopal Church, therefore, soon limited its work among Negroes to the "mere verbal instruction of those who belonged to the local parishes."[14]

The Methodists and Baptists followed suit, and the Presbyterians split on the matter, the northern body continuing to educate Negroes. The southern group, however, "fell back on the policy of the verbal instruction and memory training of the blacks that they might never become thoroughly enlightened as to their condition."[15]

Not only were the religious assemblies of slaves on plantations restricted but the colored churches which had been founded more than fifty years before were looked upon with hostility, and attempts were made to disperse them. In South Carolina the African Methodists were forbidden to meet and

---

[13] Jones, *op. cit.*, p. 115.
[14] Bowen, *op. cit.*, p. 243.
[15] *Ibid.*, pp. 243-244.

"the bishop, his exhorters and immediate followers were ordered to be imprisoned if they did not leave the state."[16]

There was also a psychological reason at work for withholding instruction from the Negroes on the part of many owners. As expressed by one contemporary observer:

> To change their general course of treatment would be virtually acknowledging to them and to all the world that they have been in error; that they have not placed them as high in the scale of intellectual and moral being as they should have done.[17]

Furthermore, there was the simple feeling of lethargy involved:

> New cares, new troubles, new duties, new expenses array themselves before us, and we recoil from them all. Changes are inconvenient, even from bad to good. . . .Their moral and religious condition may not be as bad as some would have us believe. We have been doing well in times past; apply then the adage to the case in hand, "let well alone."[18]

Similarly, a Virginia planter considered permission for slaves to learn to read and write "exceedingly impolitic" and cited in support another adage, "Where ignorance is bliss, 'tis folly to be wise."[19]

The scientists were not extremely vocal on these issues. There were, however, two self-styled ethnologists of the day who made known their conflicting opinions about Negro education. The first, Josiah Clark Nott, wrote a letter to the Freedmen's Bureau in 1865 with reference to their energetic programs of Negro education, insisting that "God Almighty made the Nigger, and no dam'd Yankee on top of the earth can bleach him." In a slightly more sober mood, he wrote the same organization the following year that

> The Bureau was the most mischievous institution ever established in this country. . . .Your great object is to elevate

16 *Ibid.*, pp. 18-19.
17 Jones, *op. cit.*, p. 109.
18 *Ibid.*
19 Quoted by Paulding, *op. cit.*, p. 194.

> the negro above the condition from which you have re-
> moved him, and to place him in every respect upon a full
> equality with the whites.

This, he insisted, was based upon an assumption contrary to
science.[20]

S. A. Cartwright on the other hand was seemingly amused
at the frantic attempts to keep enlightenment from the Negro
mind. He wrote that "experience proves that masters and
overseers have nothing at all to fear from civilized and intelligent negroes. . . ." because they are, after all, a different
species. The Negro has "a servile mind . . . almost void of
reflective faculties, and consequently unable to provide for
and take care of himself."[21] Slavery is thoroughly scriptural,
he pointed out, so there was really nothing to fear. "There
is no office which the negro or mulatto covets more than
that of being a body servant to a real gentleman."[22] Cartwright further claimed:

> There never has been an insurrection of the prognathous
> race against their masters, and from the nature of the
> ethnical elements of that race, there never can be.

He believed that all such occurrences were strictly due to
local white fanatics who stirred up the Negroes.

But, fortunately, there is an ethnological

> law of their nature which estops the evil influence of such
> characters by limiting their influence strictly to personal
> acquaintances.[23]

He was confident that the prejudice against educating Negroes
stemmed from the ideas of the abolitionists and the British
theories that "the negro is a white man with black skin."
His amusement may have been only "skin deep" however, as
revealed in his next statement, that

---

[20] Jenkins, *op. cit.,* p. 276.
[21] Cartwright, *op. cit.,* pp. 715-716.
[22] *Ibid.,* p. 718.
[23] *Ibid.,* p. 724.

if such an assumption had the smallest degree of truth in it, the more profound the ignorance and the deeper sunk in barbarism the slaves were kept, the better it would be for them and their masters.[24]

In this kind of intellectual and social climate it is easy to see, as Woodson has stated it, that "American slavery extended not as that of the ancients, only to the body, but also to the mind."[25] The alternative solution to the slaveholder's dilemma had been pressed to the hilt. As one spokesman portrayed it in the Virginia House of Delegates in 1832,

> We have so far as possible closed every avenue by which light may enter their minds. If we could extinguish the capacity to see the light, our work would be completed; they would then be on a level with the beasts of the field and we should be safe! I am not certain that we would not do it, if we could find out the process. . . .[26]

[24] *Ibid.*, p. 715.
[25] Woodson, *op. cit.*, p. 170.
[26] Quoted, *ibid.*, pp. 170-171.

5

THE ROLE OF THE ABOLITIONISTS

Another major cause of the slaveholders' tightening the
defenses of the system, in addition to the enlightenment of
the slaves through education, the potency of evangelism, and
the inflammatory literature from abroad, was the activity of
the abolitionist movement. A perusal of the literature of the
slave days strikes one with the fact that the one reference
to which pro-slavery and anti-slavery writers alike, both from
the North and from the South, reacted with criticism, sar-
casm, and condemnation was the abolitionist.

We must hasten to add that all abolitionists were not held
in such ill repute, particularly some of the earlier ones. Albert Taylor Bledsoe, an ardent slavery defender quotes one
of these, Dr. Channing, whom he calls one of "the more decent
and respectable abolitionists" as saying that the abolitionists were doing "wrong . . . frantically . . . with good intentions."[1] Dr. Channing is mentioned by another pro-slavery
writer who said that if he were still alive, Channing "would
stand aghast at the madness which is rife everywhere on this
subject."[2]

[1] Albert T. Bledsoe, "Liberty and Salvery: or Slavery in the Light
of Moral and Political Philosophy," in Elliot, *op. cit.*, 1860, p. 291.
[2] David Christy, "Cotton is King: or, Slavery in the Light of
Political Economy," in Elliot, *op. cit.*, p. 248.

The effects of the agitation of the abolitionists were seen as a real threat to men of good will from the North who were attempting to do their best for the slaves. In 1842, Charles Jones wrote about the religious revival which penetrated the South between 1829 and 1835. He described the increase of excitement in the free States over civil condition of the Negroes, with petitions to Congress and obnoxious literature "all of which had a disastrous influence on the success of the work we were attempting to do."[3] Thereafter "every movement of the Negroes was watched with jealousy. . . . Those who had undertaken the religious instruction of Negroes were looked upon with suspicion. . . ."[4]

The reader will note that the causes for Southern reaction cannot be singled out, but are interwoven. Who could identify out of the complexity of the religious abolitionist movements just which factors were viewed by the slaveholder as a threat to the complacency of the slaves? The abolitionists, no less than the defenders of the slave system, ransacked every source for arguments for their cause, which in no small measure was Bible-centered. Thus their impact was felt in the many other educational and religious efforts on behalf of the slave, and it was not always easy for the slaveholder to analyze the intentions behind each effort. Characteristically, he withdrew from anything that appeared to threaten the institution of slavery at any point.

What was the Scriptural basis for abolitionist arguments? Whereas the slavery defenders saw a divine sanction in the existence of slavery in the culture of Bible times, the abolitionists attempted to apply every possible injunction of Scripture which had anything to say about equality and brotherly love, to their ruthless insistence that emancipation *must* come *now*. They were doing exactly what Jesus and his disciples refrained from doing about slavery. Both groups missed or

[3] Jones, *op. cit.*, pp. 96-97.
[4] *Ibid.*, pp. 97-98.

ignored the Gospel's teaching that social change must come through individual change. See above, pp. 32-33, and below, p. 62.

Although it was plain to most observers that the abolitionists were sincere, and believed that they were acting in a righteous cause, their arguments suffered considerably due to exaggeration and ignorance on the one hand and poorly conceived methods on the other. Bledsoe said, "The abolitionists do not hold their passions in subjection to reason."[5] Dr. Channing, himself said that "they have fallen into the common error of enthusiasts — that of exaggerating their object; of feeling that no evil exists but that which they opposed." He denounced their "fierce, bitter, and abusive" tone and their "coarse and lacerating invective."[6]

Channing is further quoted by Barnes in 1846 as observing that the abolitionists, instead of electing

> men of strong principles, judiciousness, sobriety, . . . sent forth their orators, some of them transported with fiery zeal, to sound the alarm against slavery through the land, to gather together young and old, pupils from schools, females hardly arrived at years of discretion, the ignorant, the excitable, the impetuous, and to organize these into associations for the battle against oppression. . . .To this mixed and excitable multitude, minute, heart-rending descriptions of slavery were given in the piercing tones of passion; and slaveholders were held up as monsters of cruelty and crime.[7]

Paulding's reaction to them in 1836 was typical: "Clergymen, bachelors of arts, travellors by profession, petticoated political economists, old women, and fugitives from justice, flock among us to become our teachers in the science of humanity, and expound the mysteries of revealed religion as well as natural law."[8] He observed in another context, that since the abolitionists were instigating violence and insurrection

---

[5] Bledsoe, *loc. cit.*
[6] *Ibid.*, pp. 191-192.
[7] Quoted in Barnes, *op. cit.*, pp. 266-267.
[8] Paulding, *op. cit.*, p. 111.

among the slaves, "the people of the South are compelled, in self defense, to close up to them every avenue of religious knowledge, and to adopt all the rigorous measures of a jealous policy."[9]

Thus the abolitionist methods were deplored. "Never, it seems to me, has a good cause been more wretchedly managed in the main than the cause of anti-slavery in the U.S." This was the opinion of Albert Barnes, one of the ablest anti-slavery authors of that day. Regarding the abolitionist's methods as being "adapted to defeat," he comes to the following bitter conclusion:

> Indeed, it would seem that if Satan had resolved to employ his hightest ability in forming a scheme by which the fetters of the slave should be riveted for ever on the unhappy children of Africa in this land, he could not have devised a more effectual way. . . .[10]

[9] *Ibid.*, p. 294.
[10] Barnes, *op. cit.*, p. 266.

6

CONCLUSIONS

As the current patterns of racial segregation are examined, it is necessary to have in mind the strength and tenacity of the defenses which crystalized around the institution of slavery in reaction to the interwoven factors that have been reviewed so far.

It is likewise important to understand the significant role which these factors played in forging in the mind of the South the racial philosophy which was at once the foundation for the defense of slavery and the root from which the defense of racial segregation has grown.

Opposition to slavery precipitated social legislation designed to cope with theological, educational, economic, psychological, and legal aspects of the life and status of the Negro. The factors of opposition periodically swelled and waned. With each new increase or combination of factors, the defenses of slavery became welded more solidly. Confronted with the sagacity of the opposition, slavery grew more dogmatic; confronted with the ineptitude of the opposition, slavery grew more confident. While the opposition could change its ground, slavery, on the defensive, could only stand its ground. As its opposition matured ideologically, slavery atrophied ideologically. Finally, the strain of the legal and formal tensions broke in war, but the basis of the ideological defense system underwent no comparable alteration. The parallels apparent in the segregation system today testify to the continuity of the system.

The appeal to Scripture has been seen in the defense of slavery as well as in the attack upon it. Slavery has had to face Scripture at every turn in the form of legal, social, racial, and purely doctrinal thrusts. This has been true because the fundamental basis of slavery is a racial doctrine to which Scripture will always be opposed. Yet Scripture was woven into the very fabric of the defense system of slavery.

To see the extent to which these features and this apparent conflict can be found in racial segregation today will be the object of the remainder of this book.

Part II

SEGREGATION

INTRODUCTION

At the beginning of this study we took note of the "primary conclusion" reached by William Sumner Jenkins in his *Pro-Slavery Thought in the Old South,* that "the Southern mind was absorbed in making a defense of slavery."[1] We may now observe, by a paraphrase of this and his succeeding observation that

> The primary conclusion resulting from this study is that the Southern mind is absorbed in making a defense of segregation. The whole Southern civilization, which has many distinctive features as a way of life, is so completely identified with segregation as to make its very existence seem to depend upon the defense of that institution.

Such a conclusion is not at all a difficult one. On every hand are statements and opinions which reinforce the obvious fact. For example, a few statements from selected leaders of the South indicate that to retain racial segregation is tantamount to maintaining and perpetuating "the laws, customs, traditions, and the culture of our southern way of life" (Senator Eastland)[2]; to maintaining "the ideas of the South" (Sam

[1] Jenkins, *op. cit.,* p. vii.
[2] James O. Eastland, "We've Reached Era of Judicial Tyranny," 1955, p. 14.

50

Engelhardt)[3]; to maintaining "the Southern way of life" (Governor Talmadge)[4] and that to fail in this, "constitutes a threat to the mores of the South" and "weakens our form of government, itself" (Governor Griffin).[5] "Defeat means death, the death of Southern culture."[6]

This is not a rational identification. The defense of segregation is synonymous in the mind of the South with so many emotionally involved views that to ask that it be isolated for analysis is to expect the impossible. "It means that the average white Southern citizen, man or woman, doctor or bus driver, . . . is unalterably opposed to integration. . . . This is not a matter of sense, or morals, or reasoning, and these very same Southern citizens will admit it."[7] Most segregationists do not bother to analyze. Why should they? None of us are willing to commit our strong preferences to the cold light of intellectual analysis. Not that he couldn't have done so, but Alan Paton reported that in his interview with Governor Talmadge, "The Governor made no intellectual defense of segregation; it was simply the Southern way of life."[8]

An observation by John Bartlow Martin corroborates our conclusion about the continuity of the ideological basis for this defense system:

> Apartness of the races is a black and white thread woven into the fabric of Southern life — its social, political, sexual, cultural, economic life. Apartness is like a vine which, rooted in slavery, never uprooted but merely twisted by the Civil War, flourished and by now entangles everyone and every-

[3] Sam Engelhardt. Article distributed by Citizens' Councils of Alabama, (1957).

[4] Governor Herman Talmadge of Georgia, quoted by Alan Paton, "The Negro in America Today," *Collier's,* Oct. 15, 1954, p. 60.

[5] Governor Marvin Griffin of Georgia, personal communication, December 14, 1955.

[6] John U. Barr, Chairman of the Executive Committee, Federation for Constitutional Government. Quoted by Anthony Lewis, "Segregation Group Meets in Secret," *The New York Times,* Dec. 30, 1955.

[7] *Newsweek,* October 7, 1957, p. 33.

[8] Paton, *op. cit.,* p. 60.

thing in a suffocating net from which no one, white or black, knows how to extricate himself.[9]

He speaks of "the old ethos" which is still lived by, and very much alive.[10] It is plain to see that the same fundamental ideas — ideas about the Negro, his place in nature, what the Bible tells about him, what science tells about him, what he should and should not be allowed to have, and what he is capable and incapable of having, — are all here, and in nearly the same form and combination.

Scripture is quoted; history is misquoted. Science is flayed, faked, and "folked" out of all recognition. Legislatures and legal dodgers are working double shifts; while all the time there is almost unanimous condemnation of the hated "abolitionist," the N.A.A.C.P.

Though the N.A.A.C.P. is an interesting counterpart to the old abolitionists in various respects, principally in its role as the scapegoat for Southerners, there are at least three vital differences which bear mentioning. First, of course, the Negro is now largely carrying the ball for himself. Second, whereas we found Barnes reporting, "Never . . . has a good cause been more wretchedly managed" than the cause of anti-slavery, we find today that the anti-segregation forces are highly organized. In the words of Senator Eastland of Mississippi, "Never in the history of the United States has there been such a well planned, massive, and effectively executed propaganda barrage as that now directed against us."[11]

Third, the southern defenders do not see the chief threat merely in the organization itself, but in its dreaded backing: ". . . this thing is broader and deeper than the N.A.A.C.P."[12] A few, like "The Whiteman's Candidate," John G. Crommelin of Birmingham, believe that the Jews control the N.A.A.C.P. They are to him, the "real enemy of 'white

[9] John Bartlow Martin, *The Deep South Says "Never,"* 1957, p. 7.
[10] *Ibid.*, p. 26.
[11] Eastland, *op. cit.*, p. 6.
[12] *Ibid.*, p. 5.

Christian Alabamans'."[13]   But by far, most segregationists believe it to be the Communists who are in back of their opponents.   The logic of the argument makes it inevitable. Communists are for racial tolerance and equality; anti-segregationists are for racial tolerance and equality; therefore anti-segregationists must be influenced by Communism.   This manner of thinking was startlingly revealed a few years ago when a Christian friend of mine was approached by the colored maid in the basement of her apartment house.   The maid said to her, "It's all right, you can talk to me here; I know you're one of us."   When my friend expressed her ignorance of what was meant, the maid told her that she thought she was a Communist because she had been kind to her, and had smiled at her in the elevator!

Of course there is enough real Communist activity and influence behind the unrest to substantiate some of the claims. But these claims are little short of staggering.   In 1944 the pamphlet "The Races of Mankind," written by two outstanding anthropologists to tell the scientific meaning of race and heredity, was blocked from circulation among the armed forces, by Representative Andrew May.   A House Military Affairs Sub-Committee said the pamphlet contained "all the techniques . . . of Communistic propaganda."   In 1953 interracial marriage was tagged by Georgia Representative David C. Jones and Senator John D. Shepard as a "philosophy inspired by Moscow."[14]   And in 1954, G. T. Gillespie referred to the "worldwide movement for racial amalgamation which has its fountainhead in Moscow."[15]   Senator Eastland claims that the directors of the N.A.A.C.P. are "church groups, radical organizations, labor unions, and liberal groups of all shades of Red."   He believes with others that the Supreme Court decision on desegregation in the schools was a response to a

[13] Quoted by Harrison E. Salisbury, "Race Issue Shakes Alabama Structure," *The New York Times,* April 13, 1960.
[14] Quoted in *The New York Times,* March 1, 1953.
[15] G. T. Gillespie, "A Christian View of Segregation," 1954, p. 3.

"radical pro-Communist political movement in this country."[16]
Former Governor Griffin of Georgia states:

> It is my belief that efforts to mix the races in this country
> are communist-inspired and are solely a by-product in the
> fight to destroy our constitutional form of government.[17]

These sweeping generalizations tempt one to analyze further
their exact extent, but we must return to the consideration
of Scripture and science, and their relationships in the structure of the racial doctrine which forms the basis for the
segregationist defense system.

[16] Eastland, *loc. cit.*
[17] Personal communication, December 14, 1955.

1

SCRIPTURAL JUSTIFICATION FOR
RACIAL SEGREGATION

As with slavery, we find that the arguments from Scripture in support of racial segregation fall easily into the same four categories (see p. 12):

(a) *Segregation of divine origin; of benefit to the Negroes; the natural order.*

Supporters of racial segregation, both North and South, are certain that it is a "law of God,"[1] "the plan and purpose of God,"[2] and "in accord with the Divine Will of God as manifested in the Created Order."[3] Just as the Nazi racists believed that "each race on this earth represents an idea in the mind of God,"[4] so today the defenders of segregation evoke similar sanction for separation, imagining that "God in His divine wisdom ordained that man should maintain a pure blood stream in his own race."[5]

Expressions of the belief that segregation has benefited the Negro race are numerous. Entirely typical is that of

---

[1] Tom Brady, "Segregation and the South," *Baptist Bulletin*, 1957, p. 15.
[2] Kenneth Kinney, "The Segregation Issue," *Baptist Bulletin*, 1956, p. 8.
[3] James P. Dees, "A Survey of the Racial Issue," 1958, p. 28.
[4] Ruth Benedict, *Race: Science and Politics*, 1943, p. 54.
[5] Arkansas Baptist resolution, quoted in Campbell and Pettigrew, *op. cit.*, 1959, p. 38.

the Rev. G. T. Gillespie in an address before the Mississippi Synod of the Presbyterian Church in the U. S.:

> . . . the Southern negro has somehow managed to acquire a great number of homes, farms, banks, and other properties, has achieved a higher standard of living, and today enjoys larger educational and economic opportunities, is happier and better adjusted, than can be said of any comparable number of his race at any time in their history or in any part of the world today.[6]

We notice that such assertions always specify the "Southern" Negro, that they inevitably compare him to others of his race elsewhere in the world, and that the cause for the difference is always assumed to be the institution of segregation. The same argument was used in defense of the institution of slavery. It seems never to be realized that in many cases the same author who takes such pains in pointing out the progress of the Negro under segregation, takes equal pains to paint a dark picture of his disease, his immorality, his shiftlessness, and his stupidity. Now, the crucial point here is that whereas a *cultural* progress is described, these negative characteristics are portrayed as attributes of the *race,* when, as a matter of fact, they are products of the *same cultural tradition* which has "caused" the progress. It seems never to have dawned on white segregationists that when such inferiorities are attributed to race and offered as reason to perpetuate the system, the Negroes continue to be treated in such a way as to actually increase the symptoms which are thought to make segregation necessary in the first place! The reason for the ignorance of this process lies in failure to understand the distinction between "race" and "culture" which will be further discussed below. (See pp. 72, 73).

Arguments based upon the observation that segregation is "One of Nature's Universal Laws"[7] are just as common

---

[6] Gillespie, *op. cit.,* p. 7.
[7] *Ibid.,* p. 5.

now as they were in support of slavery, still emphasizing the difference in status of created beings. Usually they take the form of the "Birds-of-a-feather-flock-together" argument, which we shall discuss briefly later. Perhaps the last word among such opinions of the natural order of things was Tom Brady's concluding statement of an address in San Francisco in 1957:

> I now fervently say, *"Dum vivamus tum segregabimur et post mortem — deo volente, etiam nunc sic erit,"* which literally translated means, "As long as we live, so long shall we be segregated, and after death, God willing, thus it will still be!"[8]

(b) *Examples of segregation in the Old Testament*

Along with all of the parallels between the biblical defense of slavery and of segregation, there is one marked difference: whereas there are numerous examples in Scripture of the institution of slavery, there is no mention anywhere of racial segregation. That the segregationists are aware of this fact would seem to undermine their case substantially; however, we find that it does not. For, although Gillespie, for example, frankly admits that "the Bible contains no clear mandate for or against segregation as between the white and negro races," he insists (and many others have written to the same effect) that "it does furnish considerable data from which valid inferences may be drawn in support of the general principle of segregation as an important feature of the Divine purpose and Providence throughout the ages."[9] The balance of the argument always includes references to various occasions on which God separated individuals or groups, usually because of their own sin or to prevent their exposure to the sin of others.

The all-important case is that of the "segregation" in Genesis of Noah's three sons who are supposed to be the progenitors

[8] Brady, *op. cit.*, p. 15.
[9] Gillespie, *op. cit.*, p. 8.

of the three races. This is always cited, not as merely a report of their distribution or migration as it is on the face of it, but as God's pattern of keeping people apart. It is made to imply "that an all-wise Providence has 'determined the . . . bounds of their habitation.' "[10] Inference is piled upon inference, with no Scriptural basis whatever, until the proposition sounds most logical:

> Noting that each of these three groups was to keep to its own tongue and family and nation, do we not face the fact that *God* drew the lines of segregation (or separation) according to His purpose?[11]

It does not seem to matter that the migration to the south was not limited to the sons of Ham, nor that the populations involved were all of the *same race* at the time this "segregation" took place.

The remainder of examples, as has already been mentioned, do not involve race as a factor any more than the preceeding case. Nevertheless, the justification is secured by inference. Gillespie summarizes the argument as follows:

> Since for two thousand years the practice of segregation was imposed upon the Hebrew people by Divine authority and express command, and infractions of the command were punished with extreme severity, there is certainly no ground for the charge that racial segregation is displeasing to God, unjust to man, or inherently wrong.[12]

The whole argument fails to take account of the simple fact that desegregation does not envisage doing away with any other criterion for separation than that of race. Christians certainly must uphold the teachings implicit in the examples of Divine separation. To extend the implications to cover criteria for separation other than those involved in the Scriptural context, if carried to its logical extreme, would lead to ridiculous ends. On this basis, not only races but

---

[10] *Ibid.*, p. 9.
[11] Kinney, *op. cit.*, p. 8.
[12] Gillespie, *op. cit.*, p. 13.

language groups, sexes, and many other "Divinely ordained differences" should be segregated.

One other case of importance in the Old Testament, though somewhat the reverse of the previous one, is that of the Tower of Babel in Genesis 11. This case is usually used by the segregationist as indicating God's wrath upon an attempt at integration. Of course the Scripture is clear on two points: First, that God was displeased with their pride ("let us make a name for ourselves,") and second, that the population involved was probably not racially differentiated ("Behold, they are one people, and they have all one language.") Gillespie believes, with others, that the confusion of tongues at Babel "indicates that the development of different languages was not merely natural or accidental, but served a Divine purpose, in becoming one of the most effective means of preserving the separate existence of the several racial groups."[13] In seeking further bases for racial segregation, does the argument not prove, as suggested above, that God did not intend the crossing of linguistic barriers either? Perhaps this should be even more rigorously observed by man, since it receives the explicit reference and active intervention of God, while nothing is mentioned about race.

At least one pro-segregationist writer of today seems to hold, with Josiah Priest and Ariel (see p. 24), that the Tower was solely the project of Negroes.[14] According to this account, "as a result of the rebellion of the Hamites against the decree of God came the judgement of Babel."

(c) *The New Testament and segregation*

Of all New Testament references, the one most cited by defenders of segregation is Acts 17:26. The first half of this verse was, and is, used to support the argument for racial

---

[13] *Ibid.,* p. 9.
[14] Kinney, *op. cit.,* p. 9.

unity and equality: "And he made from one [blood][15] every nation of men. . . ." To this the segregationist inevitably replies, "Yes, but you haven't quoted the rest of the verse. It ends with the words: . . . 'having determined allotted periods and the boundaries of their habitation.'" This seems to clinch the argument. If God has set the boundaries for man's habitation, is it not violating God's program to mix populations together? The association of this verse with the dispersal of the progeny of Noah's sons is usually made.

One phrase in this verse, however, is always overlooked or ignored by the defenders of segregation. The verse reads:

> And he made from one every nation of men *to live on all the face of the earth,* having determined allotted periods and the boundaries of their habitation. (Emphasis is mine).

Thus an alternative interpretation is suggested, namely, that God gave man the whole earth to live on. One correspondent, replying to a segregationist article, wrote, "These two verses (Acts 17:26, 27) might better be used against those who someday expect to inhabit the planet Mars rather than applying them to the segregation of races. . . ."[16]

There is a tendency to waste time quibbling over the precise meaning of selected texts and, in so doing, to miss the larger teaching of the whole message. This is true in the handling of many controversial matters where a particular passage is made to pronounce for both sides.

In the case of slavery, we have noted that there were three main views of Scripture as it relates to that institution: Slaveholders saw examples of slavery in the Bible, found no direct condemnation of it, and considered that its overthrow would destroy the way of life of which it was a part.

Abolitionists, basing their arguments upon every Biblical

---

[15] The King James Version reads, "and hath made of one blood all nations. . . ." The Revised Standard Version omits "blood."

[16] Richard H. Mosher, letter to the editor, *Baptist Bulletin,* January, 1957, pp. 6-7.

teaching of equality and man's responsibility to man, found slavery to be sin and demanded immediate emancipation.

Christianity's effects upon the institution, however, were seen by men such as Albert Barnes as being fundamentally opposed to the basic conception upon which slavery was based — "the essential superiority of one class of men over another" — and as working a gradual rather than a sudden revolution in society which would ultimately give the death-blow to the entire institution.

In the case of racial segregation, we find almost the exact parallel in the views held by those concerned.

(i) The "Christian View on Segregation" held by the segregationists is summarized as follows:

> Since Christ and the Apostles taught the love of God for all mankind, the oneness of believers in Christ, and demonstrated that the principles of Christian brotherhood and charity could be made operative in all relations of life, without demanding revolutionary changes in the natural or social order, there would appear to be no reason for concluding that segregation is in conflict with the spirit and teachings of Christ and the apostles, and therefore un-Christian.[17]

Note how the slaveholder's view of Scripture is paralleled by that of the segregationist. We have seen that, according to this view, examples of various kinds of separation are found in the Bible; that "the Bible contains no clear mandate for or against" racial segregation; and, we note from this summary statement, that it is assumed that desegregation would constitute a revolutionary change in the natural or social order.

(ii) Those represented by the N.A.A.C.P., the most vocal Negro leaders, and the most vocal white agitators for desegregation, basing their Scriptural case upon the very same elements as the abolitionists did, demand "desegregation now."

(iii) The impact of the Gospel upon the institution of racial segregation, we submit, is exactly parallel to its impact upon

---

[17] Gillespie, *op. cit.*, p. 13.

slavery. In the first place, since one of the fundamental conceptions of segregation is the same — "the essential superiority of one class of men over another" (see p. 33), it follows
that the Bible remains as unalterably opposed to segregation
on this point as to slavery. In the second place, these teachings, together with the important consideration that they
have been increasingly supported and corroborated by science
since slavery times, are working the same gradual revolution
in our society. In the third place, insofar as the scientific
and the Scriptural teachings of racial equality coincide
it can be said that these forces are gradually accomplishing
the death-blow of the institution. Now the nature of these
forces is of consumate importance, since Scripture is inter-
preted by the segregationist to support his own case and
science (social and physical) is variously discounted or opposed. To claim, as we do, that the common ground
held by science and Christianity is the field where racial
segregation will finally fall is to invite a challenge by those
who either claim that this common ground supports the
foundations of segregation or else deny that there is any
common ground at all.

Nevertheless, we find the slow process of social revolution,
observed as the logical effect of Christianity upon slavery,
more in evidence today than ever before. This is due in
no small measure to the great increase in the common ground
spoken of before. Indeed, it is tacitly recognized by the
segregationist as the development to fear most. Thus Senator Eastland, surely more concerned with the process than
with its moving forces, sounds a warning by drawing a clear-
sighted distinction:

> The present condition in which the South finds itself is more
> dangerous than Reconstruction. . . . It is more dangerous in
> that the present Court decisions are built on gradualism. . . .
> In Reconstruction there was the attempt to force the hideous
> monster upon us all at once. . . . Its weakness then was that
> they attempted to enforce it all at once. It will take special

precautions to guard against the gradual acceptance, and the
erosion of our rights through the deadly doctrine of gradualism.[18]

Arnold Lunn similarly spoke of slavery as being "slowly
eroded by the Christian atmosphere."[19]

The change from the doctrine of "separate but equal" to
the complete removal of legal segregation in the classroom
also finds its parallel in the history of slavery.   There were
various attempts in the first half of the nineteenth century
to clean up slavery and make it "Christian" by doing away
with the abuses which were drawing the fire of the abolitionists.   Where progress of this sort was made, the biggest
abolitionist guns were silenced.   A counterpart of this "Christian" slavery may be seen in the earlier attempts to make
Negro schools equal in all respects to the white schools.
The energy in this direction on the part of the Southern States
was a major argument against the charges of the North.[20]
Here, likewise, the achievement of "separate but equal"
schools would largely have silenced segregation's most vocal
critics.   Yet, both cleaned up slavery and "separate but
equal" schools were finally superseded by the official overthrow of their parent institutions.   In this regard, note
Arnold Lunn's trenchent comment:

> The modern Christian whole-heartedly condemns slavery not
> because the academic defence of Christian slavery, as I have
> called it, is easy to refute, but because the practical experience
> of centuries has proved that it is impossible to maintain those
> safeguards which alone render slavery reconcilable with
> Christianity.[21]

No matter how "christian" were its forms, slavery itself was
founded on an ideology incompatable with Christianity. Like-

[18] Eastland, *op. cit.*, p. 7.
[19] Arnold Lunn, *A Saint in the Slave Trade*: *Peter Claver, 1581-
1654,* 1935, p. 71.
[20] See for example, James F. Byrnes, "The Supreme Court Must Be
Curbed," *U.S. News and World Report*, May 18, 1956, p. 51.
[21] Lunn, *op. cit.*, p. 68.

wise, it was finally learned, "that in the field of public education the doctrine 'separate but equal' has no place Separate educational facilities are inherently unequal."[22]

It remains now for us to examine the nature, the derivation, the similarity to slavery arguments, and the biblical and scientific bases of segregation's doctrine of inequality.

(d) *Supposed teachings regarding the Negro race*

Segregation's defense system retains a good many of the basic arguments regarding the Negro race which were incorporated into the slavery defense system. Those derived from the Bible are still centered in the person of Noah's son, Ham. In a recent (1959) publication on the subject, T. B. Maston has written, "The only reason to give any space to 'the curse of Ham' is the fact that so many people are using it today to justify the present racial pattern, just as their forefathers used it to defend slavery."[23] It is stock teaching about the Negro from far more Northern pulpits than is sometimes realized. A part of the reason is, as the segregationists alledge, that as an explanation for the derivation of the three major racial groups, it is a theory "the accuracy of which has not been successfully disputed by the anthropologists and ethnologists."[24] There are, of course, no data, anthropological, historical, or prehistoric, to disprove the claim that the Negro race is derived from the seed of Ham, any more than there are to prove it!

The present parallels with the defense system of slavery (see above pp. 16-18) line up about as follows: (a) the curse Noah pronounced upon the sons of Ham is believed to remain over his progeny forever; (b) the historic and present Negro race is presumed to constitute this progeny; (c) all "Africans" — Ethiopians, Hamitic peoples, *etc.* are considered automati-

---

[22] Supreme Court Ruling, May 17, 1954.
[23] Maston, *op. cit.*, p. 99.
[24] Gillespie, *op. cit.*, p. 9.

cally as Negroes throughout history. (d) The sinful and "rebellious" character of Ham is extended to his progeny forever; (e) the Negroes, therefore, are not to be considered the "equal" of the sons of Shem and Japheth, apart from any physical or racial considerations.

Illustrative of much of this pattern of thinking is the development of the subject by Dr. Kenneth Kinney.[25] There was a "spirit of rebellion" in the Hamites, resulting in willful crossing of the "boundaries" set by God and the Babel episode. Since God separated the three groups and intended that they should retain their identity, "the *descendants* of of these groups are, therefore, Scripturally bound to do so. Hence there should be no crossing of the line by way of intermarriage between those of Japhetic (European), Shemitic (Oriental), and Hamitic (African) groups." Kinney sees the attempts to violate this rule largely on the part of the Negroes in their attempt to become fully integrated. "Thus the Hamitic spirit of rebellion continues."

Some still refer to Cain as the original "segregated" one for killing his brother, Abel. Rabbi Arthur Gilbert even finds as one of the "most commonly uttered charges of the 'religious' segregationists" today the belief that "the sign placed upon Cain . . . was the color black. The Negro race therefore calls to mind the man who was an outcast of God and society."[26]

Thus the curse, and the continuity — "the vine . . . rooted in slavery." This branch continues to flourish.

[25] Kinney, *op. cit.*, p. 9.
[26] Arthur Gilbert, "The Bible Speaks on Segregation," *Christian Friends Bulletin*, Vol. 14, No. 2 (April, 1957), pp. 3-4.

2

SEGREGATION AND SCIENCE

From a perusal of the literature in defense of racial segregation, the treatment of matters relating to science may be seen, almost invariably, as falling into one or another of three general categories: folk beliefs, pseudo-scientific writings, and anti-scientific writings. The defense of slavery used only the first two of these since the sophistication and advancement of the science of physical anthropology, then known generally as "ethnology," was not sufficient to challenge it. Science in those days drew most fire from those who saw it as jeopardizing certain standard interpretations of Scripture (see above, p. 10). It draws the same fire today from many quarters, but, as we have already pointed out, the common ground between science and Scripture in this particular field is such that there is no longer any basic conflict.

Present and past views on racial inequality received great impetus from the writings of Comte Joseph Arthur de Gobineau, who in 1853-5 published a two-volume work entitled *Essai sur l'inégalité des races*. The pattern of thinking in this work was reflected in much of the pro-slavery literature of the times. According to Gobineau, the white race was supreme; the yellow race was next, characterized by mediocrity; and the Negro was on the bottom, a slave of blind appetite. These three were related to Japheth, Shem, and Ham, respectively. From this and other sources come many of the present beliefs in our first category, folk beliefs.

I propose under folk beliefs to discuss certain misinformation about the Negro and genetic heredity which engenders so much emotion and which has been handed down from generation to generation for hundreds of years. Taking pseudo-scientific and anti-scientific together, we shall briefly describe certain attempts by scientists to support these folk beliefs with scientific proofs and shall mention some current attempts to debunk those areas of science, as well as those scientists, which tend to undermine the segregationist defense system.

(a) Folk beliefs

The main thesis of the ardent segregationist, as it was in the case of the slaveholder, is that the Negro is distinctly inferior on many counts. Judge Tom Brady (whose little book, Black Monday, is characterized by John Bartlow Martin as "the most comprehensive exposition" of the doctrines of the white Citizens' Councils) believes mankind is divided into three distinct species; that the Negro's skull is thicker and his brain smaller than the white man's; that he has "an inherent deficiency in mental ability, of psychological and temperamental inadequacy"; that he is "non-moral," naturally indolent and indifferent by nature and has a "natural tendency to immorality and violence."[1] Vast ignorance of the distinction between what is attributable to "race," and what to "culture," is everywhere apparent in expressions of this sort. Ignorance of this vital distinction characterizes all of these categories under discussion and will be treated in more detail later.

Perhaps the most violent reaction to desegregation and the most dismal area of misinformation are in regard to inter-

[1] Brady, *óp. cit.*, pp. 6-8.

racial marriage, or "amalgamation," as it is usually called. Ignorance of the distinction between race and culture is perhaps in direct proportion to ignorance in matters of genetics and heredity. References to "pure blood lines" are simply everywhere, and whole systems of argument are based on the idea of preserving a non-existant racial purity. Editorial writers, ministers, and statesmen; rabblerousers and respectable citizens: all are instrumental in preserving the naive folklore of "mongrelization." One warns against "an impure, mixed breed that would destroy the white race."[2] Another says, "I don't want to be around to see the white race vanish and, in its place, a strange half-breed mixture emerge. . . ."[3] A Representative and a Senator from Georgia are quoted: "In the South we have pure blood lines and we intend to keep it that way."[4] Similarly a Southern judge pronounces: "We will maintain at any and all sacrifices the purity of our blood strain and race. . . . The white race shall forever remain white."[5]

Dare one hope that, after sixty years of progress in genetic science, some understanding of heredity will soon percolate to the public and that non-specialist literature will begin to sound as if the writer understood that blood has nothing to do with it? The previously quoted judge even writes that the three main races each have "different qualities, instincts, and characteristics, transmissible by descent."[6]

Stemming from the belief in "pure blood" lines are the widely held beliefs that crossing these results in racial and cultural deterioration. Gobineau wrote that wherever yellow or black mixed with white, decay resulted. In the face of all

[2] Walter B. Jones, "I Speak for the White Race," in the Montgomery *Advertiser,* March 4, 1957.

[3] From a letter to the editor, *Collier's* Magazine, Nov. 26, 1954, p. 18.

[4] David C. Jones (Georgia State Representative) and John D. Shephard (Senator), quoted in *The New York Times,* March 1, 1953.

[5] Walter P. Jones, *loc. cit.*

[6] *Ibid.*

the cultural history to prove the contrary (granted the race-culture distinction is understood), these claims continue to abound. Thus former Governor Griffin of Georgia writes:

> Throughout the course of history, it has been proved that those countries in which the populace loses its racial identity, also lose their capacity for leadership in the world and retrogress into second-rate powers.[7]

Judge Tom Brady writes in *Black Monday*:

> Whenever and wherever the white man has drunk the cup of black hemlock, whenever and wherever his blood has been infused with the blood of the Negro, the white man, his intellect, and his culture have died.[8]

With reference to physical consequences, a Southern scholar, Dr. L. L. Gwaltney, is quoted in an Alabama newspaper editorial as writing that "in amalgamation the worst qualities of both races usually appear in the off-spring."[9]

The converse of the argument is also in evidence, equally unsupported by history:

> It is a noteworthy fact that down through the centuries the most conspicuous advances in human progress have been made by those peoples, who by reason of circumstances or by deliberate preference have been isolated to a great extent from other nations and races over long periods of time, and thus have been left free to develop their own peculiar genius and distinctive characteristics and culture.[10]

Mixed marriage, in the minds of most defenders of segregation, is either the avowed and primary objective of the Negroes who desire desegregation or will be the inevitable result, desired or not. This is reflected in so many writings by Southern leaders today that it requires no documentation. In their desperation to construct arguments against segregation, however, they are sometimes caught in contradictions

---

[7] Personal communication, December 14, 1955.
[8] Quoted by Anthony Lewis, "Segregation Group Meets in Secret," *The New York Times*, December 20, 1955.
[9] Anniston *Star*, July 11, 1957.
[10] Gillespie, *op. cit.*, p. 6.

(such as Negro progress vs. poverty and disease within the segregated system referred to on p. 56). Herbert R. Sass in his article "Mixed Blood and Mixed Schools" refers to the Negroes' strong desire to elevate themselves through amalgamation, saying that this desire on their part "is only natural and human." Yet he fears that the whites' "salutary instinct of race preference which keeps the races separate, as in Nature" will be destroyed with desegregation.[11] This is the same "instinct" mentioned by Henry W. Grady long ago:

> We believe that there is an instinct, ineradicable and positive, which keeps the races apart. We add in perfect frankness, however, that if the South had any reasonable doubt of its existence it would by every means in its power, so strengthen the race prejudice that it would do the work and hold [with] the stubbornness and strength of the instinct.[12]

It would certainly appear to most observers that the South has "reasonable doubt."

The fear of intermarriage is, of course, a mixture of the belief that there is something unnatural and unchristian about it, with all sorts of folk beliefs as to the consequences. What is needed is a clear understanding that the deplorable and evil consequences are all in the social category, not the racial. The precaution to be taken is where to live and bring up the children as much as deciding whom to marry.

The fear of intermarriage, born of the impression that it is unnatural, unchristian, and physically harmful, stems in part, from the continuity of slavery thinking. Many defenders of segregation, in the North as well as in the South, today feel exactly the same about it as Josiah Priest did in 1852:

> When the two races come in contact, and the thought of amalgamation crosses the mind of a white, it is accompanied with a chill of the soul, which is nothing else but the voice of God in nature against it. . . . surely, God never intended any such jumbling up of his original work. . . .[13]

[11] Herbert R. Sass, "Mixed Schools and Mixed Blood," 1956, pp. 10-11.
[12] Quoted in Miller, *op. cit.,* p. 118.
[13] Priest, *op. cit.,* pp. 223-224.

It is not intended here to treat lightly the very real nature of the preference for one's own race in marriage. It is only intended that the negative consequences must be seen as existing solely within the society in which interracial marriage takes place; not in the marriage itself.

(b) *Pseudo-scientific and anti-scientific writings*

There is a slowly increasing number of publications devoted to an allegedly scientific defense of racism, including racial segregation. Some of them are concerned with psychological testing, such as A. M. Shuey's *The Testing of Negro Intelligence* (1958), and the *U. S. News and World Report* article, "A Scientist's Report on Race Differences" by Dr. F. C. J. McGurk.[14] As an example of the slant given the question in these publications, we may point out McGurk's attempt to prove statistically on the sole basis of intelligence tests, largely of World War I vintage, that the Negro is psychologically inferior and unable to be educated to the same degree as whites. The author denies that Negro differences from whites correlate with any socio-economic factors. Furthermore, he claims that the seven reports published between 1918 and 1950 upon which he bases his conclusions "are not a selection of studies intended to emphasize a point of view. They are the *only* existing studies that relate to the problem."[15] Of course, if the problem were considered to be strictly intelligence test scores, he could be right. But if the problem, as the title of the article implies, was "A Scientist's Report on Race Differences," then a large and vital body of literature was completely ignored.[16]

Perhaps somewhat more important than such works are those which attempt to teach racism by means of a pseudo-

[14] September 21, 1956.
[15] *Ibid.*
[16] See James O. Buswell, III, "Psychologist Claims Negroes Inferior," *Journal of the American Scientific Affiliation*, Vol. 8, No. 4 (Dec. 1956), pp. 14-15.

scientific genetics and a genetically deterministic view of history, combined with a calculated hostility towards the science which has taken the greatest strides in both areas, namely, anthropology. Let us take a closer look at the nature of this particular controversy.

One of the most significant contributions made by the science of anthropology in the past half century, hand in hand with the science of genetics, is an understanding of the intricacies of race. Genetics has provided physical anthropology with the experimental method and the understanding of the workings of genes and chromosomes which, when applied to man, resulted in an understanding of the nature of physical differences. Cultural anthropology, on the other hand, furnished an understanding of the role of culture in molding the helpless and instinctless human individual (whose behavior is learned, not given) into a member of his society. Thus, for the first time there arose an understanding, based upon concrete observation, experiment, and analysis, of the crucial difference between what the human being receives from his culture, and what is provided for him at birth through the genes of his parents. In isolating these two distinct contributions, anthropology provided the basis for discarding, once and for all, the previously held beliefs which were based upon the assumption that one's race largely determined one's behavioral characteristics, personality, mentality, and the major cultural differences of the world.

Any social philosophy or institutionalized social system whose fundamental ideology embodies the racial determinist explanation for human differences will find among its adherents those who deem it necessary to oppose the findings of anthropology. They will also oppose any advances made in the socio-psychological disciplines which encroach upon the ideological bases of their vested interests.

Racial segregation's most tenacious aspect, as we have attempted to reveal in this study, is not its capacity for physical survival, but rather for ideological survival. Having been drawn through the fire of slavery and forged upon the hearth of reconstruction, it has been firmly welded into the Southern Way of Life. It is not surprising then, that segregation's defenders, in the face of the Supreme Court's ruling of May 17, 1954, found it necessary to attack the social science theories upon which the ruling was based. These theories were largely anthropological and sociological in their dealings with race and culture in general, and with our own American Negroes in particular. The contribution of social psychology was also vital in the analysis of the consequences of segregated education.

The opposition to desegregation, then, has taken the form of debunking prominent anthropologists and their theories on race, and of decrying the socio-psychological findings which are the rationale for the revolutionary order.

Three works are noteworthy for their serious attempts to oppose anthropological theory on race. One is Byram Campbell's volume, *American Race Theorists: A Critique of Their Thoughts and Methods* (1952). Another is W. C. George's report commissioned by the Governor of Alabama in 1962, "The Biology of the Race Problem." A third is Carleton Putnam's *Race and Reason: A Yankee View* (1961). All three attack Franz Boas, the "Father of American Anthropology," and his contributions between the turn of the century and the 1940's on the understanding of race. Each shows a complete lack of understanding of the concept of "culture" in its anthropological usage. Consequently, they have not the remotest appreciation of the crucial distinction between race and culture in the formation of the individual. This places their arguments entirely within the framework of racial determinist thinking.

Putnam completely rejects "the modern equalitarian anthropology." "It is my considered opinion," he writes, "that two generations of Americans have been victimized by a pseudo-scientific hoax in this field, that the hoax is part of an equalitarian propaganda typical of the left-wing overdrift of our times, and that it will not stand an informed judicial test. I do not believe that ever before has science been more warped by a self-serving few to the deception and injury of so many."[17] The subsequent analysis of Boas' views shows a lack of acquaintance with anthropological premises and is ethnocentric at every point.

The fact that the Supreme Court looked to social science for light in which to interpret the Constitution and that they actually documented the historic 1954 ruling with the writings of social scientists, aroused a tremendous wave of criticism. Students and senators, judges and Citizens' Council members joined in with derisive abuse. A University of North Carolina correspondent to the *Daily Tar Heel* (which had, at the time, a desegregationist editor) referred to "the sociological society sitting in the Supreme Court Chambers."[18] Tom Brady called the ruling "that illegal, sociological, and unconstitutional decision."[19]

W. J. Simmons, in a lecture circulated by the Citizens' Councils, made a series of such statements. (Notice the deterioration in the terminology.) The court "takes leave of the law and starts rendering edicts based on sociology. . ." Warren "based his interpretation of the Constitution upon the writing of left-wing sociologists and psychiatrists. . ." and the court tells the Southern people "that they shall run their public schools according to the theories of certain social revolutionaries. . . ."[20]

Even former Supreme Court Justice, James F. Byrnes criticized the court for the fact that the ruling was "supported not by legal precedents but by the writings of

[17] Carleton Putnam, *op. cit.*, p. 22.
[18] Letter to the Editor, "On Liberalism," signed by Tom Turnipseed, in *Daily Tar Heel*, Nov. 5, 1957, p. 2.
[19] Brady, *op. cit.*, p. 10.
[20] William J. Simmons, "The Midwest Hears the South's Story," An Address. . . .

sociologists." They "reverse the law of the land upon no authority other than some books written by a group of psychologists. . ."[21]

One might think, from these expressions, that legal procedures were entirely outside of a social context; that legal precedent must not be colored by progress in social science!

Further examples of failure to appreciate the racial-cultural distinction are evident in virtually all segregationist literature. They take the form of claims that all the great ideas of civilization, all the worthwhile inventions, and all the arts and sciences were the achievements of white men. That the Negro developed no such civilization, written tradition, art, or science is taken as conclusive proof that his natural racial capacities were inadequate for these tasks. This subject is at the very heart of anthropology, which, in its refinement and elaboration of the concept of culture, has taken these observations out of the realm of race entirely.

The opposition of segregationists to anthropology and other social sciences is thus seen as a part of the defense system for an ideology of racial inequality which is fundamental to the slavery-segregation tradition.

[21] James F. Byrnes, "The Supreme Court Must Be Curbed," *U.S. News and World Report,* May 18, 1956, pp. 50, 54.

3

RACE AND REASON

In order to probe more deeply into the nature of the "scientific" defense of racism and to analyze better its weak points, we should look more closely at the book *Race and Reason* by Carleton Putnam. Its embodiment of the typical folk-beliefs, as well as its elaboration of the pseudo- and anti-scientific arguments provide us with a fairly complete coverage of the standard approach of the supporters of the slavery-segregation defense system.

Putnam's *Race and Reason* is a very widely heralded book on the defense of racism in our day. Newspaper reports[1] have claimed that "*Race and Reason* deserves the attention of all Americans," "is a tremendously important work," "a calm, perceptive and clarifying examination of this many-sided issue," "a blockbuster in print," "page after page of pointed and brilliant answers," "a real contribution to the history of our times," "a book that ought to be read by every thinking American, North and South," "the most important single document yet published on the question," and "one of the most important books of the day."

Senators Harry F. Byrd, Richard B. Russell, and Strom

---

[1] The quotations here cited are taken from a brochure, "Recommended Reading: A Book Headed for Fame," available from the Public Affairs Press, 419 New Jersey Avenue, S.E., Washington 3, D. C.

Thurmond have given the volume their personal recommendations as "must" reading.

Selected scientists, too, have given Putnam their whole-hearted support. Four of them — two biologists, a psychologist, and an anthropologist — state in the Introduction, "There is logic and common sense in these pages; there is also inescapable scientific validity" (p. viii). The publishers bill the book as an "all-inclusive study" which "provides authoritative facts," and as "the sharpest weapon yet forged in the fight for racial integrity."

The Straw Man of Equalitarianism

Putnam's opposition to the so-called doctrine of equalitarianism is a pure case of the erection and demolition of a "straw man." In his work, as throughout the literature of "scientific racism,"[2] there appears the implication that integrationists, modern anthropologists and all friends of the Negro race believe there are no racial differences and no individual inferiorities and superiorities. Putnam believes that not only are there such differences but he also argues for *racial* inferiorities and superiorities on this basis.

He believes that the "equalitarian" is interested in integration of the races simply because of a naive assumption that since they are all equal they might as well be integrated. This, according to Putnam, results in the integrationist attempting to give the inferior something at the expense of the superior. But "superiority and inferiority are the very essence of life and truth" (p. 103).[3] "Equalitarianism spells

[2] See, for example, *The Mankind Quarterly*, published in Edinburgh, Scotland; the writings of Putnam and W. C. George circulated by the National Putnam Letters Committee in New York City; and the many pamphlets and articles circulated by the Association of Citizens' Councils from Greenwood, Mississippi. For a thorough critique of these efforts, see Comas, 1961, and Ehrenfels, Madan, and Comas, 1962, in the Bibliography.

[3] Page references in parentheses in this section will all refer to Putnam, *Race and Reason* (1961).

stagnation and mediocrity for both." The equalitarian position "is of the very essence of this ideology to build the
inferior up by pulling the superior down."

Putnam's basic assumption here is that civilization is
genetically determined and that mixing results in deterioration. But when it is seen that culture is the major determiner
of human behavior, race becomes irrelevant, and beneficial
integration (culturally and racially) is again admissable.
The supposed deteriorating effects of integration are then
seen for what they are, namely, the consequences of cultural
antecedents rather than of racial limitations.

Far from embracing unmitigated equalitarianism, modern
anthropologists (those most severely lampooned by Putnam:
Boas, Kroeber, Herskovits, Kluckhohn, Linton, Benedict, and
Mead), and many others, hold to the very realistic position of
"not proven" in regard to correlations of behavior, intelligence,
civilization, and general culture with race. They freely admit,
indeed the bulk of ethnological research proves, that peoples
differ widely in race and culture. The argument against the
equalitarianism of modern anthropology fails to distinguish
between "equality" and "identity." Th. Dobzhansky ably
expresses the modern anthropological position in his latest
book, as follows:

> . . . the notion that all men are born not only equal but also
> biologically alike, is likewise a fallacy. . . . The mighty vision
> of human equality belongs to the realms of ethics and politics,
> not to that of biology. To be equal before the law people
> need not be identical twins.
>
> Equality means that all humans are entitled to equal op-
> portunity to develop their capacities to the fullest, not that
> these capacities are identical.[4]

Further on he states:

> Equality is a precept, similarity or dissimilarity a percept.
> Strictly speaking, science does not tell us whether people

[4] Th. Dobzhansky, *Mankind Evolving: The Evolution of the
Human Species*, 1962, pp. 13-14.

should or should not be equal, but it does show what consequences result from equality or inequality of opportunity,
given the human diversity observed. . . .

The decisive point is, however, that nobody can discover
the cultural capacities of human individuals, populations, or
races until they have been given something like an equality
of opportunity to demonstrate these capacities. . . . It does
not follow, however, that to demonstrate "equal" capacities for
cultural achievement all races will have to reproduce copies of
the civilization and polities regarded as quintessences of
enlightenment and discernment in Washington or Moscow.
Given the opportunity, they may arrange their lives in different ways.[5]

Anthropologists do not hold that there are not and never
will be genetic determiners of human behavior. Quite the
contrary, they assume that there probably are. But the simple
fact is that they cannot be isolated because of the prodigious
nature of man's learning capacity commencing at the time of
birth. This learned behavior that anthropologists refer to as
"culture" is not the sole determiner of behavior, to be sure.
It is, however, so dominant a factor that for the comparative
study of human society all other factors must be treated as if
they finally cancelled out. In an examination of the extent
to which we should assume a contribution of instinct or some
basic human nature to the similarities and diversities of human behavior, Margaret Mead concludes that

the most useful assumption seems to be that we may expect
ultimately to identify in human beings an original nature
which has very definite form or structure, and possibly
systematic individual differences which may be referred
to constitutional type within that original nature, *but
we must make our investigations without particularization in
regard to that original nature.*[6]

[5] *Ibid.*, pp. 285-286.
[6] M. Mead, "Anthropological Data on the Problem of Instinct," *in*
Kluckhohn, Murray, and Schneider (eds.), *Personality in Nature, Society,
and Culture*, 1953, p. 117. (Emphasis mine).

This is because of the overwhelming dominance of culture-historical (non-genetic) factors in the development of any civilization. Margaret Mead also observes:

> No matter how widely separated in space and time, the historical explanation becomes the only acceptable one in the discussion, for instance, of similar initiatory practices in New Guinea, Africa, Tierra del Fuego, and Australia. Each piece of cultural behavior must be referred to some historical antecedent piece of behavior, the origins of which we can never hope to examine, or test, or even profitably speculate about.[7]

Given the race-culture distinction, it follows that each piece of cultural behavior must not be referred to the race to which the individual belongs, nor to the race of his forebears.

This may be most simply illustrated by those cases in which an infant is brought up in a family of a culture and race different from that of his parents. The growing child takes on, becomes absorbed into, the *culture* of his foster parents completely in every detail of behavior, language, and values, while retaining in every detail of his own hereditary genotype the *race* of his parents.

Such cases alone would seem to invalidate many of the claims made by Putnam and his supporters that one's race sets the limits on the extent to which one's cultural development can proceed.

Putnam seems to be under the impression also that the "equalitarian anthropologists" hold that because the brain size has turned out to be an invalid criterion of intelligence, therefore all races are equal. He says:

> No one took the time to point out that not only is brain pan size not a final test of intelligence, but that, even if it were, equal brain size would not prove equal civilization (p. 23).

Again he misses completely the anthropologists' concept of "culture" as the vital factor involved and thus jumps inevitably

[7] *Ibid.*

to the wrong conclusion as to what they do hold. They certainly do not hold that equal brain size by itself allows equal capacity for civilization.

Characteristics and Qualities of the Negro

There is not an ounce more of sophistication in the folklore concerning Negro qualities in *Race and Reason* than in any of the racist propaganda one might pick up. According to Putnam,

> The Negro race has various and valuable qualities. In those great attributes of the heart — sympathy and kindness — and in a sense of humor — the average Negro, taken as an individual, is fully on a par with the average white. In certain skills the Negro ranks above the white. If I were lost in an African jungle my life might depend on the talents of a Negro. In other qualities of mind and character, qualities especially involved in our Western civilization, the full-blooded Negro is congenitally only partially adaptable (p. 36).

He quotes with approval Professor Millot, a French anthropologist, who states that

> the deficiency of the Black appears principally in logical reasoning, in judgment on the capacity to define and analyze with precision, in adaptation to new situations and in the capacity for abstraction (p. 52).[8]

Without any trepidation whatever, it may be firmly stated that this is moth-ball anthropology, if indeed it is anthropology at all.

Putnam considers the Filipino "far higher in adaptability to Western civilization than the Negro" and "the African Negro among the lowest on the scale of races" (p. 79).

It should be noted that Putnam frequently takes care to emphasize the inferiority of the "full-blooded Negro." Although he believes all inter-racial marriage contributes to the deterioration of the superior race, Putnam attributes the exceptional qualities in individual Negros to the benefits of

[8] J. Millot, *Biologie des Races Humaines*, 1952.

mixed parentage. Revealing an abysmal naiveté in genetics
for one who took a science degree at Princeton (p. 3), he
attributes the ability of "Negro doctors and other estimable
Negroes . . . to some percentage of white genes in their
system" (p. 92). He also mentions "mulattoes whose suc-
cesses are largely proportionate to the admixture of white
genes" (p. 25).

Putnam also cites blood group studies made during World
War II. According to these a hypothetical composite American Negro, the product of years of intermarriage, would be
considered 28 per cent white. Again mixing blood and genes,
he provides the following interpretation:

> It means that if all American Negro blood could be put into
> a common pool it would contain 28% white, 72% Negro,
> genes (p. 92)!

Thus the obvious superiorities of so many American Negroes
do not count at all. Putnam does not accommodate them
within his major premises because he feels safe in assuming
for them a certain degree of white ancestry. All that he
offers mulattoes is, "May God in his mercy help them to find
private solutions to their problems, but let us not mold
public policy upon a line which would increase their numbers" (p. 93).

As a home-spun philosopher of the last century, Josh Billings,
observed,

> The trouble with people is not that they don't know, but
> that they know so much that ain't so.

The "Character-Intelligence Index"

In his attempt to provide a yardstick by which to measure
different racial capacities for civilization, Putnam invokes what
he calls the "character-intelligence index." This index is
"the combination of intelligence with all the qualities that
go under the name of character, including especially the
willingness to resist rather than to appease evil" (p. 23). It
manifests itself also in contributions to great literature, en-

gineering, medicine, philosophy, and abstract science. It also
restricts certain things. Putnam specifies, "I do not include
singing or athletics as these are not primarily matters of
character and intelligence" (p. 7). He is not content
merely to say that such a pattern of cultural categories characterizes Western civilization, but he holds that the assessment
of such achievements "forms the only possible index of the
capacity for civilization as Western Europeans know it"
(p. 23). (Emphasis mine.)

Now we may ask, How is this index measured? How
does one determine which people have a high character-
intelligence index and which a low? Putnam provides us
with a ready answer. He states that "there is no test for
this index save in observing the native culture in which it
results" (pp. 23-24). Thus one is to measure the capacity
by observing the product. It is as though one were to set
up a character-intelligence index for the capacity for West
African civilization and then judge that since no white man
ever devised anything like the typical patterns of West
African culture, the white race has not the capacity to do so.

To set up criteria based upon one's own culture and then
to judge everyone else by such a standard, particularly when
it impugns their capacity for such a culture, is ethnocentric
in the extreme. Throughout the literature of which Putnam's
book is representative, contrasts between the cultural products
of the white race and those of African races are constantly
invoked in arguments allegedly proving the inherent inferiority of the Negro race. If the Negro race were indeed
inferior to the white race in any basic, genetic way, the use
of such ethnocentric and culture-blind arguments could only
serve to weaken rather than bolster the case.

Average vs. Individual Worth

In his attempt to justify racial segregation the lengths to
which Putnam's argument takes him may be indicated by
his references to the distinction between (a) the worth

and recognition of the individual, and (b) the necessity of considering only the average. At one point he lists "emphasis upon the importance of the individual" among the attributes that indicate "the capacity for a free civilization" (p. 41). At another point he lists "individualism" and "earning and deserving" among the valued concepts of the "Protestant Ethic" which he supports (p. 85). Yet concerning the possibility of judging individual Negroes on their own merits he speaks otherwise. In spite of his claim that "personally, I feel only affection for the Negro" (p. 7) and that "any American worthy of the name feels an obligation of kindness and justice toward his fellow-man [and] is willing to give every individual his chance, whatever his race" (p. 28), Putnam decides that

> in those circumstances where a race must be dealt with as a race, the level of the average must be controlling, and that the minor handicap upon the superior individual of the segregated race, if it be a handicap at all, must be accepted until the average has reached the point where desire for association is mutual (pp. 28-29).

Elsewhere he repeats that "when we are confronted with a situation where a race must be considered as a race, there is no alternative to building the system around the average" (p. 68).

What are these circumstances and situations that demand dealing with individuals only in terms of the average members of their race? Putnam would allow the individual worthy to rule "in all the ordinary judgments of life, in dealings between individuals" (p. 42), but "in those matters which involve social association, and hence the possibility of intermarrying," the individual cannot be judged on his own merits because he carries the genes of his entire racial heritage in his body (pp. 42, 68). Again the failure to understand the racial-cultural distinction precipitates an argument of undoubted logic but one based upon a false premise.

A question might be asked of Putnam at this point: What

possible "ordinary judgments of life, in dealings between individuals" might not be expected to come under "social association, and hence the possibility of intermarrying"? And
why single out marriage? In answer to the questions, "But
would Christ have discriminated according to race? Was
it not always with him a matter of individual worth?" Putnam
replies, "Of course, I have never maintained anything to the
contrary" (p. 68). But he then proceeds to make the above
exception, paying no attention to the facts that Christ never
did so discriminate, and that the questioner specified "always."
As we have observed, for the teachings of Christ racial differences are completely irrelevant.

Race and Environment

Putnam considers the contribution of the environment to
be bound by the genetic limitations of the race. "Only the
raw material was genetic. It determined the limits. What
was built within those limits depended on the environment"
(p. 27). However clear the model, the logic is invalid: the
"genetic limits" have been deduced solely from an examination
of the environmental manifestations. The reasoning thus
achieves a full circle, beginning and ending with the assumption to be proved. Thus: Negroes without aid from the
whites have not achieved Western civilization; Negroes and
whites have certain describable genetic differences; therefore
(Assumption No. 1), capacity for Western civilization must be
attributed to genetic differences.

Documentation of this point always takes for granted that
genetic variation is the single most significant causative
variable. If a more significant factor, such as culture, is
admitted, the entire system of racial superiorities and inferiorities is undermined.

Assumption No. 2 is: Since "the Negro does not have the
inborn capacity for Western civilization equal to the white
race, social integration with him invariably produces deterioration in any white civilization that tries it" (p. 106).

Documentation of this point always takes for granted the validity of Assumption No. 1, attributing all cultural deterioration to a predetermined incompatability, completely ignoring the role of cultural causation because of the limitations placed upon the role of "environment." Environment is given a place, but it is a totally cultureless environment, each race being regarded as having a genetic governor that limits its achievements. "Culture is absorbed, refined and advanced in proportion to racial capacity" (p. 27).

Putnam's discussion of this point reveals a distinct unfamiliarity with the concepts involved. He points out that the "white culture" of southern Florida differs markedly from the "black culture of Haiti, where the climate is approximately the same." From this he draws the conclusion that "the effect of the variables" (climate, and economic conditions that he seems to be putting in a non-cultural category) "is clearly less decisive than the fundamental difference in race" (p. 27). The trouble with this argument is that the difference in race is fundamental *only in a comparison of races.* If culture is the subject of comparison, race is no longer fundamental; it is, in fact, irrelevant. Putnam's basic misunderstanding of the race-culture distinction is revealed, of course, in his use of "white culture" and "black culture." Even though these terms are understood as popular phraseology, nevertheless they reflect the fundamental error in his entire argument.

Thus the end product itself, which is cultural, is used as the basis for the *argument* that civilization is genetically controlled, as well as for the *conclusion* that therefore Negroes cannot achieve anything higher than this same end product. The conclusion, argument, and premise are invalidated by the omission of the most potent of the influences molding human behavior, namely, culture.

Indeed, culture *must* be omitted from consideration by racists in order for their doctrines to stand. Putnam writes:

It is important to note that the problems of human evolution have their foundation in the physical nature of the body and brain of man and that consequently physical anthropology, not "social" or "cultural" anthropology, is the discipline primarily concerned. The genetic raw material upon which culture came to operate is the subject to be investigated.[9]

It is no wonder, then, that the position of modern anthropology has been subjected to so much critical fire by Putnam and others, for, as Professor A. L. Kroeber has pointed out, "The most significant contribution of anthropology during the first half of the 20th century is the extension and clarification of the concept of culture," with one of the chief consequences being "the toppling of the doctrine of racism."[10]

Conclusion

Mr. Putnam's two basic weaknesses, the failure accurately to assess the so-called "equalitarian" position for what it actually stands for, together with his total lack of understanding of the concept of "culture," combine to invalidate completely his entire thesis. Because of the consistency with which his arguments rely upon the resulting fallacious theory of genetics and race, the title of his book, *Race and Reason,* turns out to be wholly misrepresentative. Putnam's "race" is much more than race, involving cultural ingredients of fact as well as fiction; and his "reason" proves, upon examination from a cultural perspective, to be not only culture-blind, but circular, ethnocentric, and self-contradictory, indulging in the building and destroying of straw men in a futile effort to substantiate an argument that rests upon false premises.

Whatever arguments may be developed in favor of racial segregation under certain very unusual circumstances Putnam's book would not provide any support, for "there is . . .

[9] Putnam, "Evolution and Race: New Evidence," p. 3. See also pp. 51-52 of *Race and Reason.*
[10] A. L. Kroeber, *The Nature of Culture,* 1952, p. 139.

no possibility of studying human raciation, the process of race formation, without studying human culture . . . . Racism is . . . a relic supported by no phase of modern science."[11]

[11] S. L. Washburn, "The Study of Race," *American Anthropologist,* Vol. 65, No. 3 (June, 1963), pp. 521-531.

4

CONCLUSIONS

The defense of slavery was considered vital to the old Southern Way of Life. Slavery fell, but the "way of life" and its ideology of racial inequality continued. Racial segregation has taken the place of slavery as its cornerstone. Now, racial segregation is being seriously challenged and the South is reacting much the same as it did when slavery was threatened.

We have traced the parallels in the Scriptural bases for both institutions and have seen four things: One, examples of slavery and instructions for those concerned do appear in Scripture. Two, examples of segregation on the basis of race do not appear in Scripture. Three, the theory that the Negro race comes from Ham (with all of its implications and alleged historical consequences) appears as a fundamental aspect of both defense systems. Four, the over-all opposition of Scriptural teachings to the ideology of racial inequalities that is found in slavery and racial segregation has worked, and in combination with scientific advance is working, a slow but sure social revolution toward the destruction of each. The recognition of this inevitability was marked by the attempt to withhold all education and Scriptural enlightenment from the slaves and is evident today in the fear of the "doctrine of gradualism" and the opposition to the scientific bases of the desegregation movement.

We have traced other parallels, such as the belief in the advantage of slavery for the enslaved and of segregation for the segregated; the attempts at "Christian" slavery and at "separate but equal" schools; and the similarity of the abolitionists to the N.A.A.C.P.

We have explored the attitudes and beliefs of segregationists in the realm of science, and have found them unable to enroll science in defense of segregation.

There remains one question which can only be asked, not answered, at this point. Since the "vine" of belief in racial inequality was only "twisted" by the overthrow of slavery and continues to show a great deal of vitality today in the face of another "twisting" experience, what is likely to be its next form? What can be done to challenge it where its strength lies — in the minds of men?

Some would answer that it will never be overthrown, but will only continue twisting and growing with the changing pressures. Some say that education will certainly help.

What do the churches say? Do the social teachings of the Scriptures as they relate to the status and treatment of minority groups need to be held aloof from the findings of the behavioral sciences in the same field?

Many churches, denominations, and councils are saying No. They are applying such findings to the situation in their swiftly changing urban neighborhoods, and are proving that the integrated congregation can become a working reality.

Some, however, are so caught up with enthusiasm for integration that they are overdoing a good thing. We deplore the position of those who teach or imply that unless one integrates one is "not Christian." Despite a distinctly anti-segregation emphasis, this book does not advocate integration simply for integration's sake. It is conceivable that racial integration in some congregations could cause more problems than it would solve.

Nevertheless, it has often been observed that the most

segregated hour of the week in the United States, north and south, is eleven o'clock on Sunday morning. Many churches choose to ignore this fact — complacently, strategically, or apprehensively where the prospect of integration or relocation is imminent. The numerous expressions of dread from those in the latter situation indicate, among other things, the vast extent to which the racial-cultural distinction has not yet become a part of the thinking of American churchmen.

I have every respect for the position of pastors faced with the dilemma of mixing or moving, just as I have for that of white families in southern counties where they are outnumbered by Negro populations of a largely different social or economic class. No pat solution can be offered. No formula can be applied to all cases. Without the particular details of each separate case, no responsible authority could venture an answer to the question, "Well, what would *you* do?" The only suggestions which *can* be urged upon all are to keep in mind that the teachings of Scripture emphasize the worth of the individual himself and nowhere suggest the relevance of his race. Remember that one's individual worth, whether more or less than that of another, is the product of his cultural learning and his spiritual relation to God — not of his race.

Another important consideration for churchmen, particularly those who approve of integration in general but criticize integrationist procedures, is that, in spite of appearances, "congregation-breaking" and "neighborhood-breaking" incidents do not represent the ultimate aims of the Negro. He is fighting for acceptance in his native culture and the strategies of conquest often outreach the ultimate objectives of victory. "D" Day did not initiate a permanent conquest of Europe. It was one stroke against the enemy in a much larger context. Certain strategies of the N.A.A.C.P. and of other organized movements should likewise be seen in the light of much larger, and in a sense, more limited objectives. They should not be criticized as ends in themselves.

Thus we submit that church and community problems should be analyzed and their solutions planned in the light of an understanding of (a) the nature and causes of racial and cultural similarities; (b) the nature and causes of racial and cultural differences; and, most important of all, (c) the crucial distinction between racial differences and cultural differences.

With greater social and scientific awareness, the ministry can collaborate with the social and behavioral sciences on their common ground. This will achieve a much greater impact upon the social thinking of our times and the times that lie ahead.

BIBLIOGRAPHY

Aptheker, Herbert, editor, *A Documentary History of the Negro People in the United States;* from Colonial Times Through the Civil War. New York: Citadel Press, 1951; Paperback ed., 1962.

Ariel (B. H. Payne), *The Negro: What Is His Ethnological Status?* Cincinnati, 2nd ed., 1867 (1st ed., 1840).

Auer, J. Jeffrey, editor, *Antislavery and Disunion,* 1858-1861; *Studies in the Rhetoric of Compromise and Conflict.* New York: Harper & Row, 1963.

Baldwin, S. D., *Dominion: or, the Unity and Trinity of the Human Race; with the Divine Political Constitution of the World, and the Divine Rights of Shem, Ham, and Japheth.* Nashville, 1858.

Barber, Jesse B., *Climbing Jacob's Ladder. The Story of the Work of the Presbyterian Church, U.S.A., Among the Negroes.* New York: Board of National Missions, 1952.

Barnes, Albert, *An Inquiry into the Scriptural Views of Slavery.* Philadelphia: Perry and McMillan, 1846.

Benedict, Ruth, *Race: Science and Politics.* New York: Viking Press, 1943; Paperback ed., 1959.

Blaustein, Albert P. and Clarence Clyde Ferguson, Jr., *Desegration and the Law; The Meaning and Effect of the School Segregation Cases.* New York: Vintage Books, Random House, 2nd ed., 1962.

Bledsoe, Albert T., "Liberty and Slavery: or, Slavery in the Light of Moral and Political Philosophy," *in* Elliott, ed., 1860.

Bowen, Trevor, *Divine White Right. A Study of Race Segregation and Interracial Cooperation in Religious Organizations and Institutions in the United States.* New York: Harper, 1934.

Brady, Tom, *Black Monday.* Winona, Miss.: Assn. of Citizens' Councils, 1955.

———, "Segregation and the South." Greenwood, Miss.: Citizens' Councils Educational Fund, 1957.

Breckinridge, Robert J., "The Black Race: Some Reflections on its Position and Destiny as Connected with Our American Dispensation," A Discourse delivered before the Kentucky Colonization Society at Frankfort, Ky., Feb. 6, 1851. Frankfort, Ky.: A. G. Hodges and Co., Printers, 1851.

Brown, Edward, *Notes on the Origin and Necessity of Slavery.* Charleston, S. C.: Printed by A. E. Miller, 1826.

Burmeister, Hermann, *The Black Man. The Comparative Anatomy and Psychology of the African Negro.* New York: W. C. Bryant and Co., Printers. 1853.

Buswell, James O., III, "Psychologist Claims Negroes Inferior," *Journal of the American Scientific Affiliation,* West Lafayette, Indiana, Vol. 8, No. 4 (Dec. 1956) pp. 14-15.

Byrnes, James F., "The Supreme Court Must be Curbed," *U. S. News and World Report,* May 18, 1956, pp. 50-58.

Cable, George Washington, *The Negro Question. A Selection of Writings on Civil Rights in the South.* Edited by Arlin Turner. New York: Doubleday, 1958.

Campbell, Byram, *American Race Theorists: A Critique of Their Thoughts and Methods.* Boston: Chapman and Grimes, 1952.

Campbell, E. Q., and T. F. Pettigrew, *Christians in Racial Crisis: A Study of Little Rock's Ministry.* Washington: Public Affairs Press, 1959.

Carroll, Charles, "The Negro a Beast" or "In the Image of God." St. Louis: American Book and Bible House, 1900.

Cartwright, S. A., "Slavery in the Light of Ethnology," *in* Elliott, ed., 1860.

Christy, David, "Cotton is King: or, Slavery in the Light of Political Economy," *in* Elliot, ed., 1860.

Clarke, Walter, "The Anti-Slavery Society at War with the Church," A Discourse delivered before the First Congregational Church and Society in Canterbury, Conn., June 30, 1844. Hartford, Conn.: Elihu Greer, 1844.

Cobb, Howell, *A Scriptural Examination of the Institution of Slavery in the United States,* [Perry?], Georgia: Printed for the author, 1856.

Comas, J., " 'Scientific' Racism Again?" *Current Anthropology,* Vol. 2, No. 4. (Oct. 1961), pp. 303-340.

Dees, James P., "A Survey of the Racial Issue," *The Defender* Nov., 1958, pp. 28-33 (reprinted as Defender Pamphlet No. P — 117).

Dobzhansky, Theodosius, *Mankind Evolving: The Evolution of the Human Species.* New Haven: Yale University Press, 1962.

Douglass, H. Paul, *Christian Reconstruction in the South.* Boston: Pilgrim Press, 1909.

Du Bois, W. E. B., *Darkwater,* New York: Harcourt, Brace and Howe, 1920.

Dykeman, Wilma, and James Stokely, *Neither Black nor White.* New York: Rinehart, 1957.

Eastland, James O., "We've Reached Era of Judicial Tyranny," Greenwood, Miss.: Citizens' Councils Educational Fund, 1955.

Ehrenfels, U. R., T. N. Madan, and J. Comas, "*Mankind Quarterly* Under Heavy Criticism," *Current Anthropology,* Vol. 3, No. 2 (April 1962) pp. 154-158.

Elliot, E. N., editor, *Cotton is King, and Pro-Slavery Arguments*. Augusta, Ga.: Pritchard Abbott, and Loomis, 1860.

Ewart, David, *A Scriptural View of the Moral Relations of African Slavery*. Revised and Amended edition, Charleston, S. C.: Walker, Evans and Co., 1859.

George, W. C., "The Biology of the Race Problem." Report prepared by Commission of the Governor of Alabama. New York: National Putnam Letters Committee, 1962.

Gilbert, Arthur, "The Bible Speaks on Segregation," *Christian Friends Bulletin*, Vol. 14, No. 2, (April, 1957), pp. 3-6.

Gillespie, G. T., "A Christian View of Segregation," Greenwood, Miss.: Citizens' Councils Educational Fund, 1954.

Grossack, Martin M., editor, *Mental Health and Segregation*. New York: Springer, 1963.

Grosvenor, Cyrus Pitt., *A Review of the "Correspondence" of Messrs. Fuller and Wayland on the Subject of American Slavery*. Utica, N. Y.: Published at the Christian Contributor office. 1847.

Harper, C., "Slavery in the Light of Social Ethics," *in* Elliot, ed., 1860.

Harris, R., "Scriptural Researches on the Licitness of the Slave-Trade, Shewing its Conformity with the Principles of Natural and Revealed Religion." London: Printed for J. Stockdale, 1788.

Hodge, Charles, "The Bible Argument on Slavery," *in* Elliott, ed., 1860.

Holly, A. P. B., *God and the Negro: . . . . or, the Biblical Record of the Race of Ham*. Nashville: Natl. Baptist Publication Board, 1937.

Jenkins, W. S., *Pro-Slavery Thought in the Old South*. Chapel Hill: University of North Carolina Press, 1935.

Johnson, Guion G., "The Ideology of White Supremacy, 1876-1910," in Green, F. M., *Essays in Southern History*. The James Sprunt Studies in History and Political Science, Vol. 31, 1949.

Jones, Charles C., *The Religious Instruction of the Negroes in the United States*. Savannah, 1842.

Kardiner, Abram, M. D., and Lionel Ovesey, M. D., *The Mark of Oppression; Explorations in the Personality of the American Negro*. Cleveland and New York: Meridian Books, World, 1962.

Karon, Bertram P., *The Negro Personality; A Rigorous Investigation of the Effects of Culture*. New York: Springer, 1958.

Kinney, Kenneth, "The Segregation Issue," *Baptist Bulletin*, October, 1956, pp. 8-9.

Kroeber, A. L., "A Half-Century of Anthropology," *Scientific American*, Sept., 1950. Reprinted in Kroeber, A. L., *The Nature of Culture*. Chicago: University of Chicago Press, 1952.

Logan, Rayford W., *The Negro in the United States: A Brief History*. Princeton: Van Nostrand, 1957.

Lunn, Arnold, *A Saint in the Slave Trade: Peter Claver, 1581-1654*. New York: Sheed and Ward, 1935.

Martin, John Bartlow, *The Deep South Says "Never."* New York: Ballantine Books, 1957.

Maston, T. B., *Segregation and Desegregation: A Christian Approach.* New York: Macmillan, 1959.

McCaine, Alexander, "Slavery Defended From Scripture, Against the Attacks of the Abolitionists," A Speech Delivered before the General Conference of the Methodist Protestant Church. Baltimore, 1842.

McGurk, F. C. J., "A Scientist's Report on Race Differences," *U. S. News and World Report*, Sept. 21, 1956, pp. 92-96.

McKitrick, Eric L., editor, *Slavery Defended: The Views of the Old South.* Englewood Cliffs, N.J.: Spectrum Books, Prentice-Hall, 1963.

Mead, Margaret, "Anthropological Data on the Problem of Instinct" *in* Kluckhohn, Murray, and Schneider (eds.), *Personality in Nature, Society, and Culture.* 2nd ed., New York: Knopf, 1953.

Miller, Kelly, *Race Adjustment: Essays on the Negro in America.* Third edition, New York: Neale Publishing Co., 1909

Myrdal, Gunnar, *An American Dilemma: The Negro Problem and Modern Democracy.* New York: Harper, 1944.

Olmsted, Frederick Law, *The Slave States (Before the Civil War)* Edited, with an Introduction by Harvey Wish. New York: Putnam, 1959.

Paton, Alan, "The Negro in America Today," *Collier's* Magazine, October 15, 1954, pp. 52-66.

Paulding, J. K., *Slavery in the United States.* New York: Harper, 1835.

Priest, Josiah, *Bible Defense of Slavery: and Origin, Fortunes, and History of the Negro Race.* Fifth edition, Glasgow, Ky.: W. S. Brown, 1852.

Putnam, Carleton, *Race and Reason: A Yankee View, Washington*: Public Affairs Press, 1961

———, "Evolution and Race: New Evidence." Pamphlet. New York: National Putnam Letters Committee, n.d.

Ramsay, James, "An Essay on the Treatment and Conversion of African Slaves in the British Sugar Colonies." London: J. Phillips, 1784.

Rose, Arnold, *The Negro in America.* Condensed version of Myrdal's *An American Dilemma.* New York: Harper Torch Books, 1964; and Boston: Beacon Press, 1956.

Rozwenc, Edwin C., editor, *Slavery as a Cause of the Civil War.* Boston: D. C. Heath, 1949.

Sass, Herbert R., "Mixed Schools and Mixed Blood." Greenwood, Miss.: Citizens' Councils Educational Fund, 1956.

Seabrook, E. B., *Ariel Refuted. A Complete Exposure of a Pamphlet Entitled "The Negro."* Charleston, S. C.: John Russell, 1867.

Shuey, A. M., *The Testing of Negro Intelligence.* Lynchburg, Va.: J. P. Bell Co., 1958.

Simmons, Wm. J., "The Midwest Hears the South's Story," An address given in Oakland, Iowa, Feb. 3, 1958, Greenwood, Miss.: Citizens' Council Educational Fund, 1958.

Snyder, Louis L., *The Idea of Racialism; Its Meaning and History.* Princeton, N. J.: D. Van Nostrand, 1962.

Stanton, William, *The Leopard's Spots; Scientific Attitudes Towards Race in America, 1815-59.* Chicago: University of Chicago Press, 1960.

Stringfellow, Thornton, *Slavery: Its Origin, Nature and History Considered in the Light of Bible Teachings, Moral Justice, and Political Wisdom.* New York: J. F. Trow, 1861.

Taylor, Thomas J., "Essay on Slavery; As Connected with the Moral and Providential Government of God; and as an Element of Church Organization." New York: Published for the author, Joseph Longking, Printer, 1851.

Tillson, Everett, *Segregation and the Bible.* Nashville: Abingdon, 1958.

Thompson, Thomas, *The Trade in Negro Slaves on the African Coast in Accordance with Humane Principles and with the Laws of Revealed Religion.* 1772.

Tussman, Joseph, editor, *The Supreme Court on Racial Discrimination.* New York: Oxford University Press, 1963.

UNESCO, The Race Question in Modern Science: *Race and Science.* New York: Columbia University Press, 1961.

Van Evrie, J. H., *White Supremacy and Negro Subordination; or, Negroes a Subordinate Race and Slavery its Normal Condition.* Second edition, New York: Van Evrie, Horton and Co., 1867.

Washburn, Sherwood L., "The Study of Race," *American Anthropologist,* Vol. 65, No. 3 (June 1963), pp. 521-531.

Woodson, C. G., *The Education of the Negro Prior to 1861.* New York: Putnam, 1915.

Woodward, C. Vann, *The Strange Career of Jim Crow.* New and Revised Edition. New York: Oxford Univ. Press, 1957.

Young, Robert A., *The Negro: A Reply to Ariel.* Nashville, Tenn.: J. W. M'Ferrin and Co., 1867.

Ziegler, Benjamin Munn, editor, *Desegregation and the Supreme Court.* Boston: D. C. Heath, 1958.

INDEX